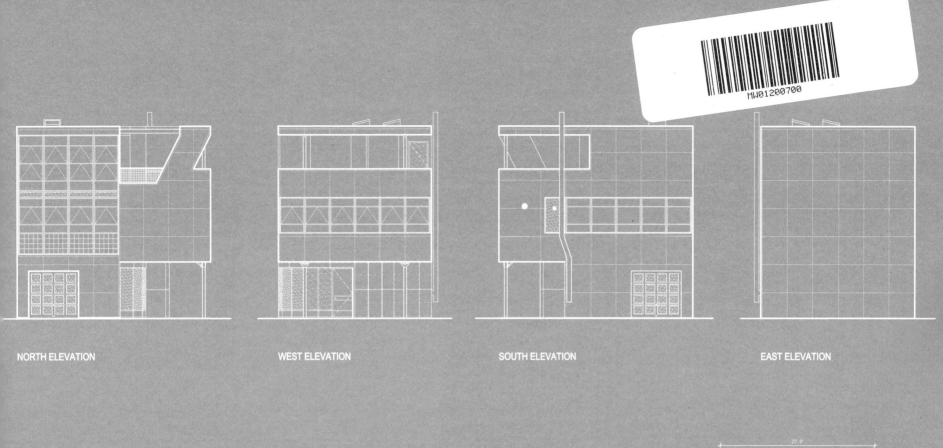

NORTH ELEVATION

WEST ELEVATION

SOUTH ELEVATION

EAST ELEVATION

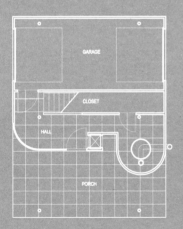

FIRST FLOOR PLAN

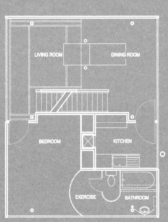

SECOND FLOOR PLAN

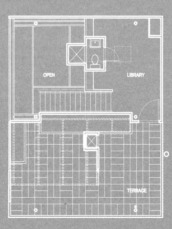

THIRD FLOOR PLAN

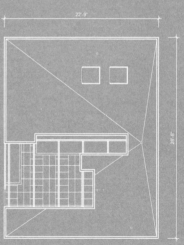

ROOF PLAN

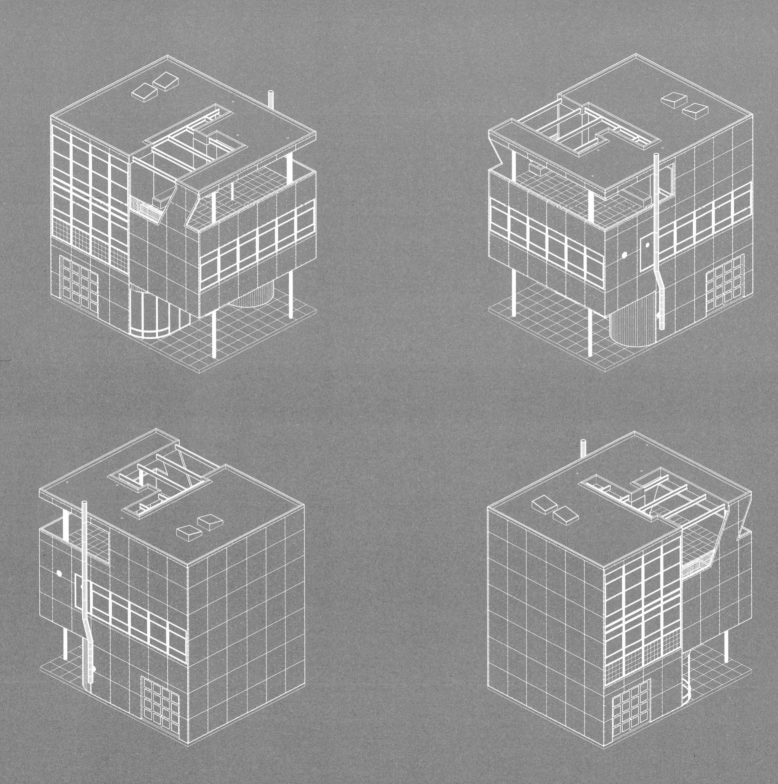

THE ALUMINAIRE HOUSE

THE ALUMINAIRE HOUSE

Jon Michael Schwarting

Frances Campani

Gibbs Smith

First Edition
28 27 26 25 24   5 4 3 2 1

Published by
Gibbs Smith
570 N. Sportsplex Dr.
Kaysville, Utah 84037
1.800.835.4993 orders
www.gibbs-smith.com

Designed by Sheryl Dickert
Printed and bound in China

This product is made of FSC®-certified and other controlled material

Library of Congress Control Number: 2023952116
ISBN: 978-1-4236-4869-7

Contents

In 1929, Lawrence Kocher, architect, then managing editor of the *Architectural Record* magazine, was asked by the manager of the Allied Arts and Building Products Exhibition, held in New York's Grand Central Palace, to design an interesting feature that would attract the general public. He chose a Modern Architect's Office.

The project was very successful, and, in 1930, Kocher was asked again to come up with something original.

I had been working with Lawrence since my arrival in the USA in early September of that year.

Knowing the American public's desire for single residential housing and the economy of prefabrication, we proposed to exhibit a Metal House that would have these features.

The name ALUMINAIRE was a catchy acronym we created representing aluminum and the desirability of Light and Airiness.

—Albert Frey, January 1997

Aluminaire House has a place in history way beyond its aesthetic and structural innovative qualities. Comparatively ignored in its day, it is important to the history of architecture as being the first built example of what we at the Museum of Modern Art have named the International Style.

Its variegated history since then has been told in other places, but from the point of view of ourselves, the instigators of the Museum of Modern Art show of 1932 and the authors of *The International Style* book of the same year, it is a beacon on a dark night. It represented the possibility of American participation in a movement which since that day has had repercussions throughout the entire world.

It is the one built evidence of the beginning of that strong and still dominant mode of American building.

—Philip Johnson, May 1996

Preface

The Aluminaire House carries within its metal structure an almost century-old tale of fame, abandonment, and rescue. As a showpiece of the 1931 annual exhibition of the Architectural League of New York City and the Allied Arts and Industries, it was a unique mock-up of a modern affordable house. Designed by A. Lawrence Kocher, an architect and editor, and Albert Frey, a young architect who had recently arrived from Switzerland, this mostly metal and glass building was proclaimed "a house for contemporary living" (see fig. 1.1).

After the exhibition, it was rebuilt on Long Island as a weekend house, and its meaning as a prototype for affordable housing was mostly forgotten, although images of the house were exhibited in the Museum of Modern Art's first exhibition on modern architecture in 1932. The house then disappeared from public awareness until the late 1980s when, under threat of demolition, it was dismantled and re-erected as a museum at New York Institute of Technology's Central Islip campus on Long Island. But in 2005 the campus closed its architecture program, and the house was once again without a home.

Figure 0.1 Advertisement for the Architecture and Allied Arts exhibition in the *Brooklyn Daily Eagle*, April 17, 1931.

Figure 0.2 Drawing by Albert Frey of the Aluminaire House during the design.

Ownership of the house was transferred to the Aluminaire House Foundation in 2011. The House was dismantled and put into storage in 2012, with a plan to relocate it to a site in Sunnyside, Queens, New York, alongside projects by Henry Wright and Clarence Stein. However, community opposition put a stop to that idea.

The Aluminaire House Foundation gave the Aluminaire House to the Palm Springs Art Museum in 2020. Palm Springs, California, is where the majority of Albert Frey's work is located. It was decided that the house would be located at the southern end of the museum property, along the road leading to Frey House II, also donated to the museum's collection. Reconstruction started in the summer of 2023 was completed in early 2024, and has been included in the museum's major Albert Frey exhibition of 2024.

Why so much fuss about such a simple, inexpensive structure? In sum, the Aluminaire House is connected to the significant cultural and historical moments and movements of its time. Its uniqueness lies in that it brought together seemingly contradictory conditions within a single building. The distinctions between early and late modern, European and American, progressive and conservative, social and visual (form and style), as they relate to the general discourse in architecture and housing, are all found in this house. Other significant architectural issues such as style, prefabrication production, and community (urban versus suburban) were also part of the conceptualization of the house and became models upon which other architects and designers experimented.

This book explores the entire trajectory of the Aluminaire House—from its inspiration and realization through its full and involved history—along with the architects who were involved with it. It also visits the social and cultural conditions that have evolved over the lifetime of the house, and how the house has been perceived throughout its years by the architectural profession and the public. Fortunately for all of us, the efforts to save this building have been successful, and its legacy will live on.

1

THE ALUMINAIRE HOUSE—1931

THE IDEA AND THE EXHIBITION

At one point in 1930, looking ahead to the April 1931 Architectural League and Allied Arts and Industries exhibition, Walter T. Sweatt, its codirector, sought ideas from architect A. Lawrence Kocher on how to make the exhibit of building products more lively.[1] Kocher, at the time managing editor of *Architectural Record*, suggested making a full-scale house that would employ new, standardized parts.[2] Intrigued by his own idea, Kocher then decided to take on the project and he hired Albert Frey, a young Swiss architect who had just arrived in New York, to work on the project with him.

The Aluminaire House, as the architects named their project, would be a celebration of modern life. Standardized parts were already being used in construction, and such components had been displayed at the building industry exhibitions for several years.[3] But for the most part, the forms of building had not changed with the methods of construction. The Aluminaire House would not hide the new parts, nor would it mimic conventional construction. Instead, the new technique of assembling "off-the-shelf" parts would be evident in this low-cost dwelling, and even overtly suggest a different way of living (see fig. 1.1).

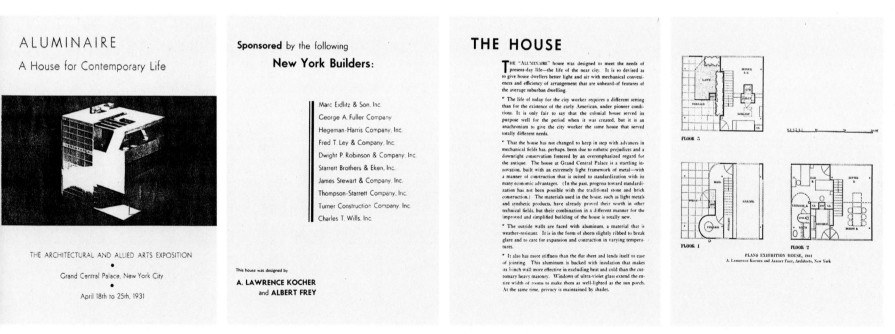

Figure 1.1 Announcement of the Aluminaire House exhibit in the Architecture and Allied Arts Exhibition, April 1931.

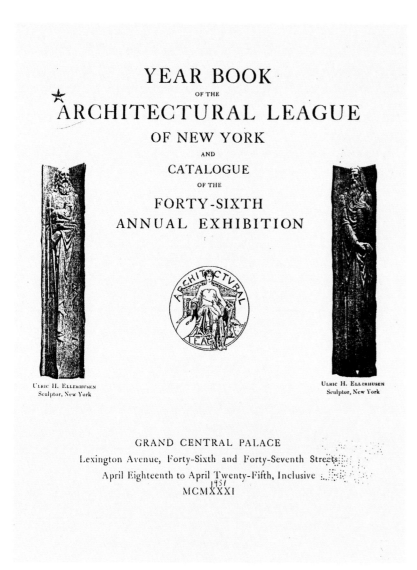

YEAR BOOK
OF THE
ARCHITECTURAL LEAGUE
OF NEW YORK
AND
CATALOGUE
OF THE
FORTY-SIXTH
ANNUAL EXHIBITION

ULRIC H. ELLERHUSEN
Sculptor, New York

ULRIC H. ELLERHUSEN
Sculptor, New York

GRAND CENTRAL PALACE
Lexington Avenue, Forty-Sixth and Forty-Seventh Streets
April Eighteenth to April Twenty-Fifth, Inclusive
MCMXXXI

Figure 1.2 The Architectural League of New York *Year Book* cover.

The Aluminaire House as a repeatable unit was part of Kocher and Frey's concept dating from at least March 1931, if not from the beginning of the project. An article by Kocher and Frey in the April 1931 *Architectural Record* challenged conventional zoning configurations and suggested the use of repeatable units. The article (coinciding with the exhibition date) not only questioned the aesthetics of the conventional house, but also proposed the reorganization of street blocks to form alternative public spaces in the community (see fig. 2.3).

Grand Central Palace, New York City.

What did the visitor to the exhibition of April 18–25, 1931, encounter in the Grand Central Palace[4] (see fig. 1.3)? Historically, the exhibits were divided into three categories. The first consisted of architectural projects chosen by the Architectural League Committee (see fig. 1.2). This was a rather conservative selection, taken from the works of well-established firms along with some international examples (including ones from Mexico and Sweden), all presented in photographs and models. It was this selection that led Philip Johnson to launch an alternative exhibition of "Architects whose work was rejected by the selection committee of the Architectural League," and caused Alfred Barr, in 1932, to refer to the exhibition as the "annual circus of the Architectural League."[5]

ABOVE: Figure 1.3 Grand Central Palace (1911–1963), Lexington Avenue and 46th to 47th Streets. This was New York City's primary exhibition space, to be replaced by the Colosseum at Columbus Circle and the present Jacob Javits Convention Center.

BELOW: Figure 1.4 Aluminaire House model built by Albert Frey to show to product manufacturers and suppliers.

The second segment comprised the decorative arts. Entries were as varied as a mural by Diego Rivera and a thirty-foot-high polychrome Zeus.

The third and last category was the Allied Arts and Industries section, with building products featuring items such as new roofing materials and overhead garage doors. It was probably as exciting to the layman as pages in Sweet's Catalog.[6]

Among this jumble of art objects, building gadgets, and stylistically dusty architecture in model form, stood the shiny, full-scale Aluminaire House—something between a domestic-size skyscraper and a giant metal canoe. In other years, a visitor to the exhibition might have skipped over the building products segment altogether, but the Aluminaire House,

though a few feet shy of Zeus in height, brought great interest to this usually ignored part of the show. The challenge to building conventions and aesthetics was put forward in the most understandable terms: a single-family dwelling unit—everyone's most intimate relationship to architecture—ready to be occupied.

While the Aluminaire House profoundly affected the Architectural League exhibition of 1931, the exhibition also profoundly affected the house. Since the 1931 exhibition was to take place in the vast Grand Central Palace, the general feeling is that the exhibition space of the Palace itself dictated the size and footprint of the Aluminaire House.[7] This constraint, however, does not account for the three-level solution the architects came up

with for the single dwelling unit. The origins of those features harken back to the precedents Kocher and Frey knew from Europe.

Notably, the most important influence of the exhibition on the House was in terms of its design development. Through the use of a model (see fig. 1.4), Kocher and Frey carried on a dialogue with the many manufacturers who supplied the materials for the house. The manufacturers produced shop drawings, translating the architects' initial ideas into materials that could be quickly assembled on the site. Having to put the house together on-site in ten days forced Kocher and Frey not only to use standardized parts, but to make the whole thing work, kit-like, inside and out.

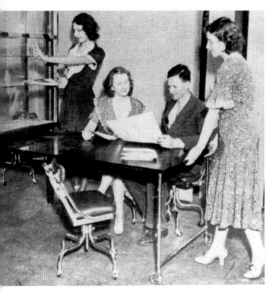

LEFT: **Figure 1.5** Albert Frey and Grand Central Palace secretaries at the Aluminaire House's expandable dining table.

CENTER: **Figure 1.6** View of the Aluminaire House entry at the exhibition.

RIGHT: **Figure 1.7** Construction of the entry to the Aluminaire at the Grand Central Palace exhibition.

OPPOSITE

Figure 1.8 Article in *Popular Science*, July 1931.

The final design demanded that the viewer understand how the house worked—from the pattern of screws and seams on the exterior elevations, to the folding furniture, the exposed boiler in the foyer space, and the exposed beam-girder-column connections. The structure is the most apparent in the most public space of the house, the living room. Kocher and Frey did not let the "workings" disappear for the exhibition (see figs. 1.5–1.7).

The structural system, and the sequencing of construction, was also affected by the fact that the House could have no foundations in the exhibition space. Without its enclosing walls, the house resembled Le Corbusier's *Maison Dom-ino* diagram[8] (see figs. 1.17, 1.18, 1.41, and 2.5).

The idea of enlivening the building products display within the League exhibition succeeded beyond the expectations of any of its initiators. Philip Johnson's "Rejected Architects" exhibition—shunning the New York status quo represented by the Architectural League—could not top this stunning commercial display located in the middle of the enemy camp. It was difficult to convince the public that the Architectural League was regressive when the headlines talked daily of its "House of the Future."[9]

The Aluminaire House was the focus of virtually all the popular press on the exhibition. Journalists used the house to speculate about the future and possible changes to one's "way of life." Newspaper articles contained both praise and objections to the new life suggested by the Aluminaire House. The exhibition was also reviewed in professional and trade journals such as *Parnassus*, *Creative Art*, *Shelter*, *Glass Digest*, as well as in *The New Republic*.

The *Brooklyn Daily Eagle* championed "the magic house of today" as "a full-sized house built without bricks, mortar, wood or nails, furnished and equipped to meet the most advanced ideas of the Homeowner."[10] The following day, the same newspaper propelled the house from the present to the future: "House of Future . . . eliminates cellar, is suspended from aluminum girders, has changeable rooms made by movable partitions."[11] The *New York Herald Tribune* also placed the house ahead of its time: "Metal Houses offered as Homes of Future"[12] (see fig. 1.10). The *New York Times* reported that the house was "all-metal" and could be rapidly constructed: "Whole sub-divisions of like houses could be put together before the basements of ordinary homes could be completed."[13] Later that week, the still cautious *New York Times* reported the total attendance at the exhibition as 135,000, and noted that the "all-metal" house was the chief point of interest[14] (see fig. 1.9).

PLANS HOMES OF ALUMINUM AND GLASS

At left, proposed model home of the future with aluminum walls and glass through which the ultra-violet light can pass.

Below, Albert Frey, New York architect, is showing how the sheets of aluminum should be attached to walls of the house.

WILL the suburbanite of the future sit in his living room behind walls of aluminum, while sunbeams stream in through ultra-violet-transmitting glass? Two New York architects thus vision the ultra-modern home in the suburbs. A model three-story house built along the modernistic lines they propose was exhibited recently in New York City to a group of architects.

The outside wall is of sheet aluminum, backed with insulating material, only three inches thick. The metal is slightly corrugated to prevent reflection of sunlight.

A seventeen-foot window of special glass, which transmits ultra-violet light, occupies one entire side of the two-story-high living room. At night, neon tubes like those used in advertising signs supply illumination. Floors and beams are of steel throughout the house.

A library on the top floor, lighted by skylights, has a ceiling of aluminum foil. The rest of the upper story is given over to a sleeping porch and an inclosure that can be used for sun bathing.

ARCHITECTS' SHOW VISITED BY 100,000

Eight-Day Exposition Here Ends With a Record for One Day's Attendance.

500 PUPILS SEE EXHIBITS

Metal House, Which Will Receive Outdoor Tests, Said to Have Been a Chief Point of Interest.

More than 100,000 persons visited the Architectural and Allied Arts Exposition at Grand Central Palace, which was closed last night after having been in progress eight days.

The total attendance was estimated at 135,000 by Walter T. Sweatt and Charles H. Green, executive directors of the show. The attendance has closely approached that of the three previous biennial architectural expositions in Grand Central Palace, although these remained open two weeks. The attendance on Friday is said to have been the largest ever recorded during a single day at an architectural show here.

Yesterday morning a group of 500 public school children visited the exposition under the guidance of the School Art League. They were shown through the displays by Ely Jacques Kahn, chairman of the exposition, and the Swedish and Mexican exhibits were explained to them by Professor Ivar Tengbom, Swedish delegate to the exposition, and Federico Mariscal, Mexican delegate.

Throughout the exposition the metal house has been one of the chief points of interest. Yesterday afternoon visitors were waiting in line to enter and explore its interior. The structure has a steel frame, with walls of aluminum, insulated against heat and cold...

A. Lawrence Kocher, who, with Albert Frey, designed the building, said yesterday that after the close of the exhibition the house would be reconstructed outdoors and its practicability thoroughly tested. The site for the house has not been decided upon yet.

ABOVE: Figure 1.9 Article in the April 26, 1931 *New York Times*.

RIGHT: Figure 1.10 Article in the April 19, 1931 *New York Herald Tribune*.

INDUSTRY
AVIATION
AUTOMOBILES

NEW YORK Herald Tribune

SCIENCE
FEATURE ARTICLE
RADIO NEWS—PROG

SUNDAY, APRIL 19, 1931

...um House at Architects' Show Marks New Build...

Model Structure Designed to Harmonize With Modern Mechanical Progress

Metal and Glass Dwelling of Ultra-Modern Conception Built for League Show

Home Built in Full Size

Equipped With New Ideas for Contemporary Living

By Lloyd Jacquet

Man must have sensed a keen enjoyment when he contemplated his first crudely built house fashioned of sticks, hides and grass. It was his creation, erected in record time as construction work goes nowadays, even in the simplest cases.

Today man stands before a modernized version of this early shelter. Instead of saplings, aluminum beams; animal skins replaced by metal sheeting; glass supplanting grass; these are the things out of which the contemporary house—built in one of the main exhibits of the Architectural League show in Grand Central Palace last week—is made of.

No mere model, this. Instead, a full-size, three-story building, erected complete from plans in a little more than a week; equipped with a practical garage, an interesting living room, a different kitchen, and an unusual bedroom, besides a sun-terrace and a small library that can be turned into another room. Practical in the extreme, but not freakish—merely convenient and common sense.

Metallic Framework

As one sees the framework with its sturdy aluminum beams interconnected with the shining columns that support the entire structre, the ensemble of angle-irons, steel floors, metal staircases, window casements, and perforated uprights give the impression of the interior of a dirigible in construction. As the men at work assemble the various numbered units as the workers on skyscrapers do, one gathers the impression that they are enjoying this quite as much as they did putting together the structural toy of their boyhood days.

Visitors will see the effect of this rapidly executed conception of a contemporary home. From the outside, though there will not be much opportunity to get the full effect within the exhibit hall, the impression is striking. Aluminum metal facing, slightly ribbed to break the glare and to accommodate contraction and expansion in various temperatures, gives it a certain massiveness free from heaviness. A thin insulation basks this aluminum sheeting, and the whole is hung from the framework. This aluminum, and the glass of the windows that are plentiful in all but one facade, provide the only exterior surfaces.

No Basement Provided

Though there was no possibility for a cellar on the exhibition floor in any case, this presented no problem, for the house itself when finally erected at some point on Long Island after it has been dismantled following its display here, will also be built without a basement. The heating system and the garage are placed on the ground floor, and the cost of excavating is thus saved.

This places the main living rooms above the ground level. This part of the house is reached by means of a short flight of stairs, and, because of its position, receives all the light and air that is needed. Extending across the width of the house and with one end glazed from floor to a ceiling height of seventeen feet, a clever duplex effect is achieved which increases its practicability.

At the other end is a dining-area which can, if desired, be converted into additional living-space. The dining-table when not in use may be contracted to the dimensions of a side table. This is done by means of an ingenious construction: the table-top, which is rubber-surfaced, is made to roll on a cylinder in the manner of a window-shade. This large room is illuminated by neon lighting, with tubes that parallel the head of the window so that with reflectors the night-lighting in its source corresponds to daylighting.

By the turn of a dial one can obtain a clear white light that suggests the quality of daylight or an ultra-violet light or a selection of color.

Located to the right of this living-room combination, and separated by a folding partition are the bedroom, exercise room and bathroom. With the partition swung back, one has the effect of a window running the entire length of the side—22 feet long.

This layout permits of an intensely individualistic arrangement of units. For example, the two beds suggested are placed at right angles to each other; the closets are small, but distinctly masculine or feminine, as the case may be. Although there are actually three rooms here, one room may be made out of this multiple-room suite, with the attendant advantages of ample space for circulation and enjoyment.

There is a door access to the dumb-waiter for sending the laundry bag to the lower floor. The dressing-table is built against the wall and is supported by brackets. It has its justified place under the window where there is a most advantageous light. The mirror placed in front of the window reflects a shadowless face. The moving partition between bed and exercise-room follows a curved line, in order to make the exercise-room more spacious.

The man sitting all day in his office finds in this exercise room the necessary apparatus for gymnastic compensation. A cabinet of aluminum-framing with translucent panels incloses the closet. It is ventilated directly to the exterior with forced draft by a vent pipe with electric fan. The bath tub is partly hidden beyond this toilet cabinet. The wash basin is placed under the window with the mirror in front of it, to again attain a shadowless lighting.

Above the dining space is the library, it occupies about half the area of the living room and is lighted by skylight, which was chosen as most desirable and restful for reading. The room is furnished with a couch, a built-in bookcase, a wall case, also for books. The library leads onto the roof terrace.

More than half of the ground area covered by the house is regained by means of a flat roof which serves as a luxurious garden terrace. This roof garden is partly covered and partly open

Walls and Floors Hung From Metallic Framework, Like Skyscraper Construction

No Basement Is Provided

Multiple-Purpose Rooms Increase Layout Facilities

to the sky. Here one can enjoy sun or shadow, take a sunbath in complete privacy and sleep under the stars on warm summer nights. Under the covered part is placed a dining table adjacent to the dumb-waiter, which brings the food direct from the kitchen below. This table may be folded up and put out of the way when the entire terrace space is required for dancing, games or as a play space for children. A radio connection supplies music. The terrace floor is covered with resilient asphalt tiles—an ideal paving for playing children. Under the part open to the sky is a sunny patch of green grass, unframed by spacious flower boxes, which, with their colorful combinations, contribute to the making of the terrace, one of the most livable places of the house. The architects have not hesitated to expose the roof framing above the roof garden. The structural channels necessary for the construction are exposed in a truthful manner in contrast with the usual pergola beams of wood used on many picturesque old-home imitations. The supports for the terrace roof frame the view in three directions.

First All-Metal House

The house is built with exterior walls of aluminum (the first all-metal house attempted in America) and has insulation that makes the three-inch thick exterior more effective than the usual 13-inch wall of masonry. The house is constructed of materials readily available as standard and in a manner that is a complete departure from tradition. It neglects all of the styles of the past in the attempt to attain convenience, ease of living, attractiveness of outlook and a logic of quiet and pleasant existence. It is as if architects had entirely forgotten the manner of building of the past centuries and were interested in creating a needed American house that would be most efficient and with most appropriate materials.

There are no supporting outside walls, as is the case with the usual brick-dwelling. The supports are six slender columns of aluminum that are within the area of the house. These columns uphold cantilever beams from which the outside walls are suspended. It is a new construction that has many advantages. The windows may come where they are needed for daylighting the interior. Inside walls may be placed where wanted.

The structure of the house is largely of aluminum beams or girders that in turn support the deck floor, insulated and surfaced with the rubber and linoleum flooring. To be sure, the house is fireproof and of extreme lightness. Even though the entire construction members were of steel, the total weight would be one-twelfth the weight of the usual house built with concrete and steel.

Conceived for present-day living requirements, this house, designed and erected under the supervision of A. Lawrence Kocher, architect, disregards all orthodox methods of construction. It is one of the features of the Architectural League Show, which opened in New York yesterday.

Other journals allowed themselves to speculate on the impact the unconventional house would have on its occupants' way of life. "Housewife may soon order more rooms by telephone and have them delivered parcel post—kitchen of the future will be dust proof."[15] The imagination of the journalists often went beyond the actual features of the house, which perhaps helped to spark the public's interest and imagination. The exhibit seemed to have caught the attention of "everyman" in a way that no other League presentation had done before. A few months after the close of the exhibition, the Aluminaire House was even the subject of an article in *Popular Mechanics*[16] (see fig. 1.11).

It is striking, given the amount of publicity the Aluminaire House received in general, that more professional journals did not cover its design and construction in the exhibition in any detail—not even *Architectural Record* where Kocher was an editor. Only *Shelter*, a more radical journal, edited by Buckminster Fuller, reproduced photographs of the exterior of the house in the Grand Central Palace, and by the time the relevant issue was published in May 1932, the house had already been reconstructed on Long Island[17] (see figs. 3.7–3.10).

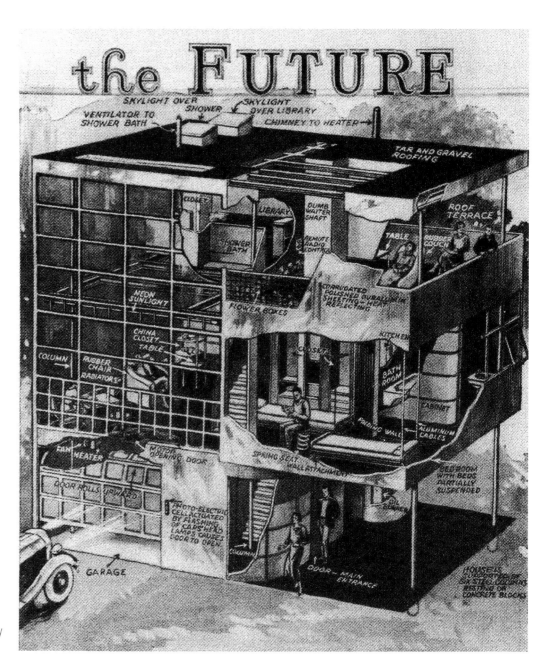

Figure 1.11 Image from "Home of the Future," an article in *Popular Mechanics*, September 1932. "Cut-away representation of the House of the Future" drawing by Logan U. Reeves. This is a good explanation of the Aluminaire House.

DESCRIPTION OF THE ALUMINAIRE HOUSE

The three-story house has a small footprint: 22 feet 6 inches wide by 28 feet 9 inches deep by 27 feet 3 inches tall (see figs. 1.15 and 1.16). Six aluminum columns of 5-inch diameter, heavy-duty pipe support girders of paired channels 7 inches deep of aluminum or steel. These are bolted at the column connections with hexagonal gusset plates (five bolts per connection). Beams spanning the girders are flush, connected with bolted angles, and are either aluminum or steel. The location rationale of the two materials is that the steel is utilized where hidden in the floor construction, while aluminum is exposed, with minor exceptions. The reason for this is not known, but cost or material availability may have influenced this decision. The structural flooring is 18-gauge interlocking steel decking, 6 inches by 1 ½ inches, called "battleship decking" at the time (see fig. 1.13). It was covered on top with a one-inch layer of wood fiberboard sound insulation and a light gray linoleum finish floor throughout.

The exterior walls are hung from the floor structure with steel angles. The walls are made of 2-inch, perforated steel angle sections as girts (see fig. 1.12). Wood dowels were initially conceived, but were later replaced with 2 by 2-inch wood nailers on which ½-inch insulation board panels were attached on both sides.

The construction predates present insulation products. On the exterior face, building ("tar") paper and aluminum panels were attached to the wood nailers with aluminum screws and washers. A colored cotton fabric with a "pyroxlin" (nitrocellulose) coating produced by DuPont (beginning in 1930) called "Fabrikoid" is the interior wall and ceiling surface throughout[18] (see fig.1.14). The interior partitions are similar to the exterior walls, utilizing the same metal girt, insulation panel, and Fabrikoid finish in a fixed, washable color.

OPPOSITE

UPPER LEFT: Figure 1.12 Wall construction section drawing by Albert Frey. A 3-inch exterior wall with early form of insulation.

LOWER LEFT: Figure 1.13 Image of the floor construction from *The Modern House* by F. R. S. Yorke, 1934.

RIGHT: Figure 1.14 Advertisement brochure for DuPont's Fabrikoid.

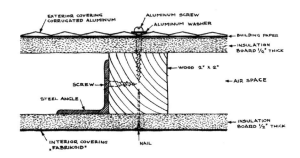

EXTERIOR WALL CONSTRUCTION

A. LAWRENCE KOCHER
ALBERT FREY

4 PARK END PLACE
FOREST HILLS, L. I., N.Y.

The following illustrations show various constructional methods for LIGHTWEIGHT ROOFS AND FLOORS and WALLING SYSTEMS developed in America and on the Continent.

1. SHEET STEEL DECK. The first use of steel deck for floors is said to have been made in the Aluminaire House in 1931 (page 181). Spans of 3 to 4 feet over open steel bar, or other steel joists are economical; sheet cork is laid over the steel deck to insulate against heat, cold and sound transmission, and to assist the equal distribution of loads. Linoleum forms the finished wearing surface (diagram below).

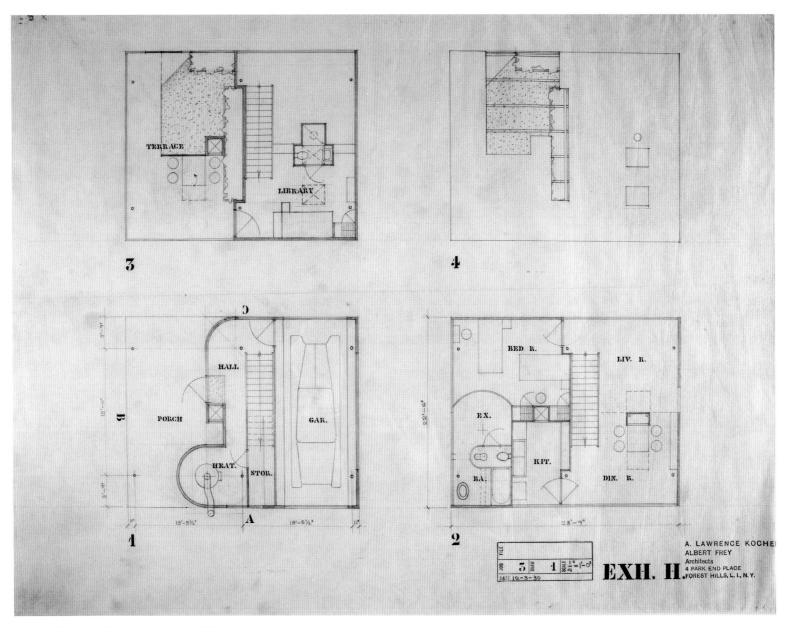

Figure 1.15 Plans by Albert Frey, October 8, 1930.

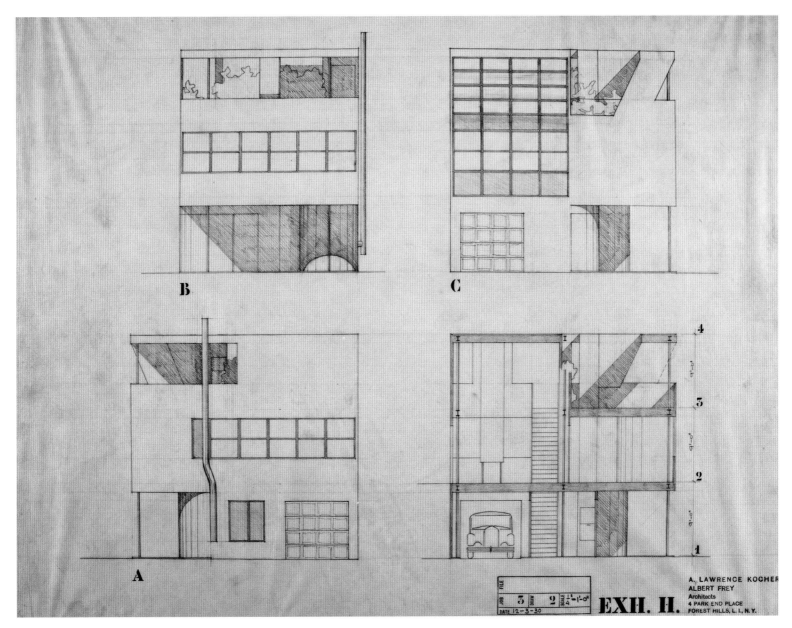

Figure 1.16 Elevations and section by Albert Frey, December 8, 1930.

The house fundamentally works on a module of 3 feet 8 ½ inches, which is the spacing of the beams, the span of the flooring, and the spacing of the exterior aluminum wall panels. The windows are steel projecting sash and tie directly into the girt spacing. The aluminum panels overlap both horizontally and vertically. Thus the screw pattern relates directly to the girt module, with the wood "nailer," to which the panel is screwed. The panel seams form their own 3 foot 8 ½ inch grid shifted horizontally off the grid to form the overlap. The panel edges and the screws form a tartan grid pattern, which is most evident on the façade of the house with no windows (see fig. 1.42, numbers 15 and 16).

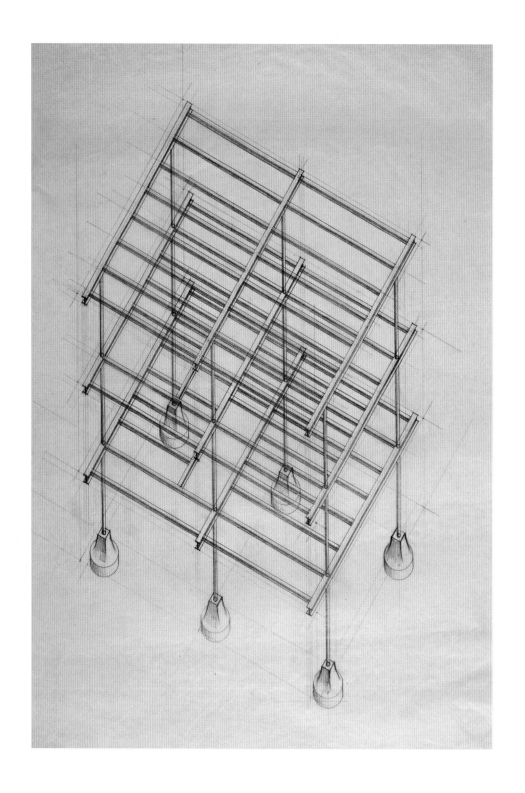

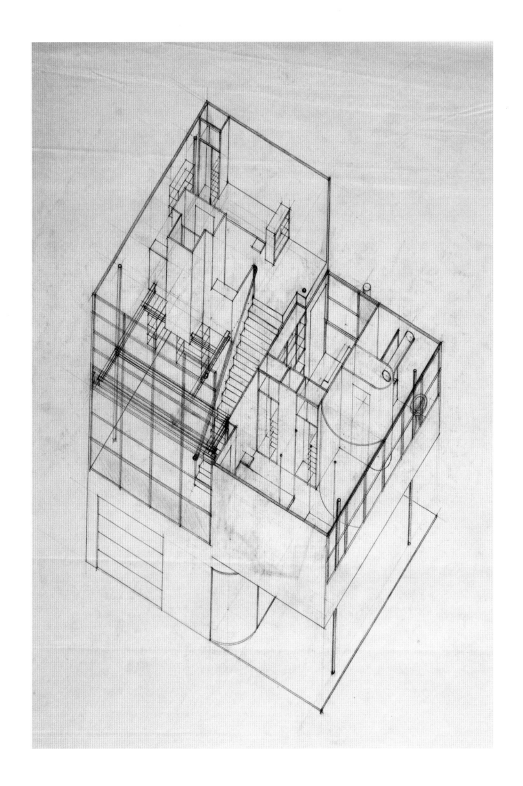

OPPOSITE: **Figure 1.17** Structural frame drawing by Albert Frey.

Figure 1.18 Cut-away axonometric drawing by Albert Frey.

Entry on the ground floor is through an open, covered terrace (see fig. 1.6) with a pair of exposed columns. The inside wall of the terrace is complex, with a front door leading into the foyer, a curved window wall, a rectangle containing a dumbwaiter, and an aluminum-sheathed semicircular form housing the boiler, openly displayed as a mechanical sculpture (see fig. 1.19). On the other side of the foyer, a door opens to the rest of the ground floor: a drive-through garage with overhead doors at each end (one automatic). From the foyer one can view a horizontal parapet at the top of the stairs giving view to the ceiling of the double-height second floor.

The foyer stairs, with a solid diagonal parapet, rise parallel to the entry terrace. The top of the stairs opens to the dining room on one side with a door to the kitchen on the other. The dining room flows directly into the living room, separated by a glass cabinet. The three-foot-wide cabinet, suspended from two chrome columns containing plumbing pipes, also houses an expandable dining table (see fig.1.20). With its rubber top, the table can be rolled out to accommodate six people. A view of the table in the exhibition shows office-type chairs on wheels, which complement the dynamics of the table (see fig. 1.5). The living room is double height and has a full width and height window wall. From the living room, the third-level library is visible over its parapet. A third-level bathroom shower projects into this double-height space (see fig. 1.21).

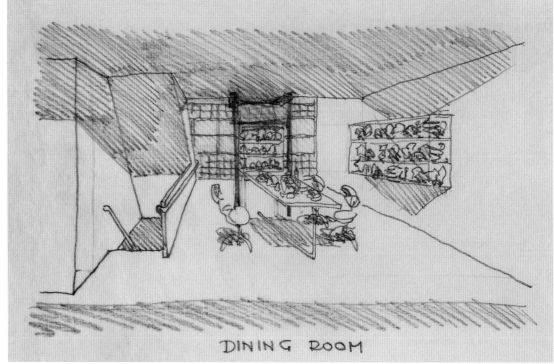

DINING ROOM

LEFT: Figure 1.19 View of the entry and boiler from above: cut-away axonometric study by Albert Frey. The boiler was to be celebrated as an art object in a semicircular niche.

RIGHT: Figure 1.20 Dining room with stair arriving from below. The glass case and roll-out table are visible, with living room beyond, Albert Frey.

Figure 1.21 Living room, dining room, and stairs to library mezzanine: a study of space and colors, Albert Frey.

MONEL , WALLS ALUMINUM

ABOVE: **Figure 1.22** Kitchen with colors, Albert Frey.

RIGHT: **Figure 1.23** Kitchen with details, Albert Frey.

On the other side of the central stair wall on the second floor, and above the entry terrace, are the kitchen and the bedroom. The galley-type kitchen boasted then-modern equipment, such as a stove with an electric clock that would automatically turn on the morning coffee. Counter surfaces are of monel (stainless steel) and cabinets are metal and glass (see figs. 1.22 and 1.23). The walls were publicized as "soundproof."[19] The dumbwaiter, at the end of the kitchen, links the lower-level entry porch and foyer and the upper roof terrace with the kitchen.

KITCHEN

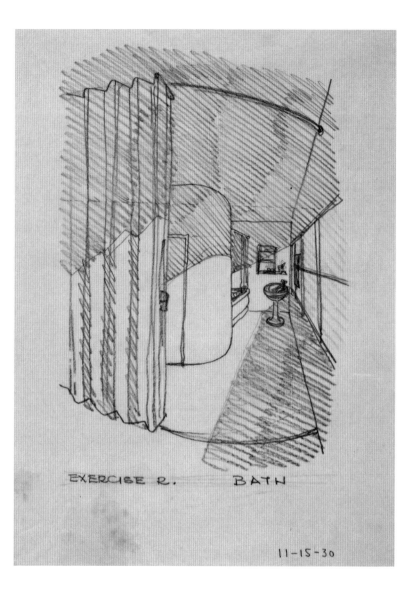

EXERCISE R.   BATH

11-15-30

The bedroom with an open bathroom runs the width of the building, behind a continuous strip window on the front façade (see fig. 1.26). The wall shared with the kitchen has a built-in efficient closet with extendable hanging racks and shelves.[20] The beds were to be suspended by rods from the ceiling to facilitate cleaning. Between the bedroom and the bathroom is an exercise area defined, for privacy, by a semicircular folding curtain connected to a top and bottom track (see figs. 1.24–1.26). In the bathroom, the toilet is enclosed in an aluminum grid and Lumarith translucent plastic panel booth with a door (see fig. 1.25). A bathtub with a Vitrolite synthetic stone surround is located behind the toilet, and the sink is freestanding at the front façade window.

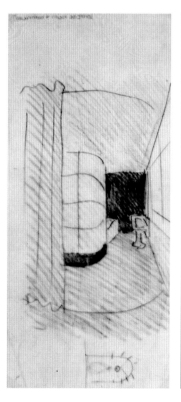

ABOVE: Figure 1.24 Bedroom with exercise area and bathroom, Albert Frey.

RIGHT: Figure 1.25 Exercise area and bathroom, Albert Frey.

FAR RIGHT: Figure 1.26 Bedroom, axonometric view from above, Albert Frey.

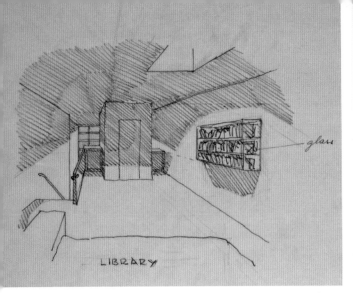

LIBRARY

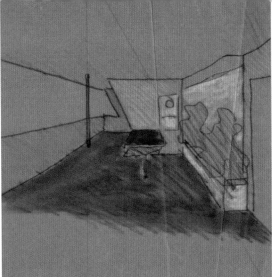

6/10/30

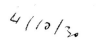

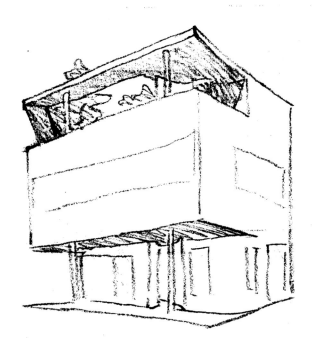

ABOVE

LEFT: Figure 1.27 Library mezzanine and bathroom looking over the living room, Albert Frey.

CENTER: Figure 1.28 Roof terrace with dumbwaiter and fold-up table. The two angled walls align visually, Albert Frey.

RIGHT: Figure 1.29 Roof terrace views from the "lawn" area, Albert Frey.

Figure 1.30 Sketch studies of the roof terrace form by Albert Frey, October 4, 1930. Albert Frey said he wanted the corner to be more open after making the sketch on the left.

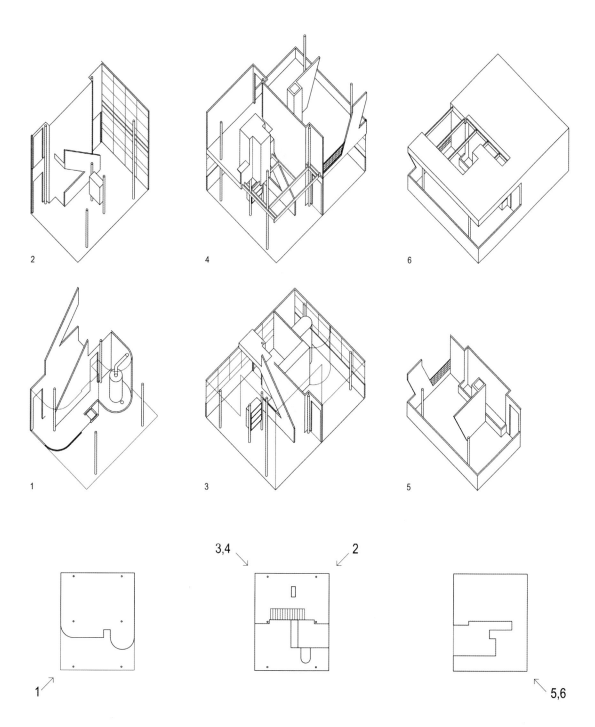

The stairway, with a solid parapet facing the living room, rises to the third level library/study that could double as a guest bedroom, and which looks over bookcase parapets back to the living room and out the double-height window (see fig. 1.27). A small bathroom, located on the edge of this mezzanine floor, is centered between the bookcase parapets. Two small square skylights, one in the library and the other in the bathroom, add light. A glass door leads to the roof terrace.[21] The terrace is partly roofed, corresponding to a paved area with a planted open area, that the original plans labeled "lawn." The dumbwaiter, adjacent to a fold-down table on an angled wall, services the terrace (see fig. 1.28). This diagonal wall aligns with the signature diagonal wall on the side elevation (see fig. 1.29). Albert Frey designed this diagonal wall to make the roof "appear to float" (see fig. 1.30). The two columns that are visible at the ground-floor entry are again exposed on the terrace in the view from below (see fig. 0.2).

Figure 1.31 Diagrams of the sequence of spaces:
1. Entry/foyer/mechanical, 2. Dining/living, 3. Living/dining, 4. Living/dining/bedroom/bathroom, 5. Roof terrace, 6. Roof.

Along with its use of new, standardized components for the structure and sheathing, the Aluminaire House also challenged conventions in its fittings. The main living spaces are lit by a seventeen-foot-high window wall. This window was to be equipped with neon lights, running continuously in a trough along the window head, that could be adjusted to provide different colored lighting approximating daylight, as well as purportedly benefiting one's health through an infrared ray light. Throughout the house, furnishings were built-in and often adjustable in order to maximize space within the small dwelling unit. Frey designed a lamp/mirror combination that could be pulled from the wall at the bathroom sink. With the lamp on, the light would radiate from behind the mirror, producing no shadows on the face (see fig. 1.34). Shelves were to be mounted on the wall in the dining room and library (see figs. 1.20 and 1.27). The glass cabinet and roll-out table, previously mentioned, were part of a publicity campaign for the house when Walter Sweatt sent three secretaries with their chairs to pose with Albert Frey. That picture is the sole remaining photographic image of the house interior from the exhibition (see fig. 1.5).[22] The mechanism for the table was not built for lack of time (see fig. 1.32). The table on the roof terrace could fold up to make room for other activities on the terrace (see fig. 1.33).

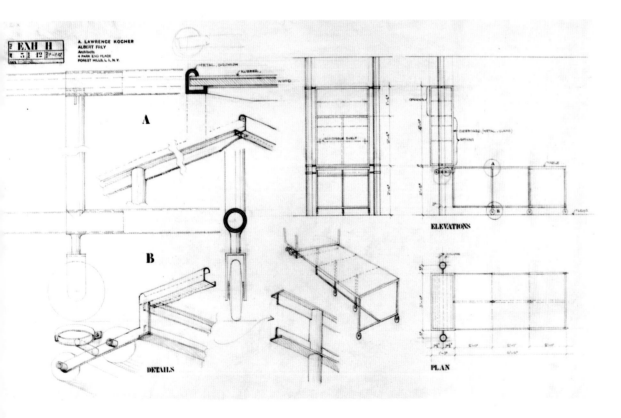

Figure 1.32 Expandable dining table. Albert Frey said that it didn't work in the exhibition. Albert Frey drawing, December 31, 1930.

OPPOSITE

LEFT: Figure 1.33 Terrace folding table. Albert Frey drawing, March 2, 1931.

RIGHT: Figure 1.34 Bathroom mirror and lamp on the column next to the sink. Albert Frey drawing, February 26, 1931.

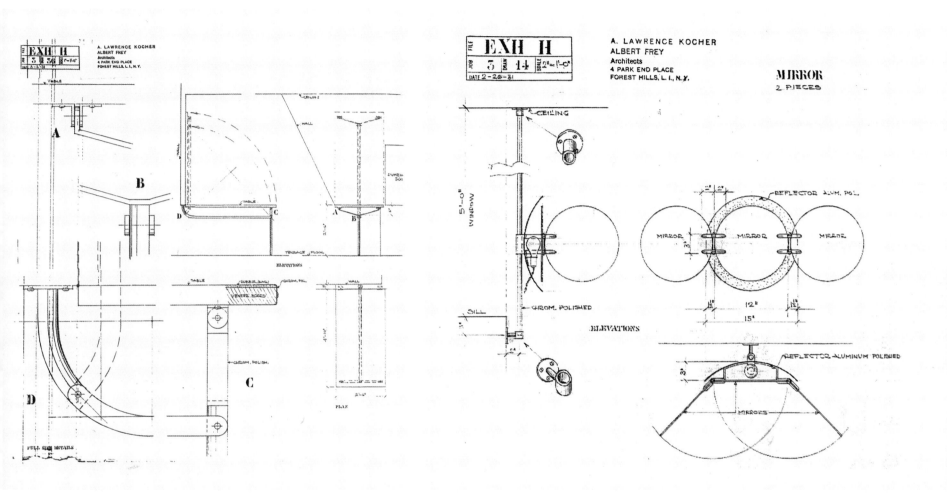

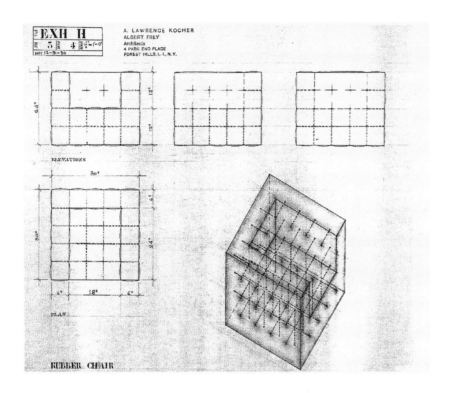

Frey also designed furniture for the house. These designs, like the plans, sections, and elevations of the house, are titled "EXH H" (exhibition house), in the standard stencil lettering used in Le Corbusier's office. The furniture included inflatable seating that looked like Le Corbusier and Charlotte Perriand's *grande confort* chairs, as well as two stools and a table (see figs. 1.35–1.39).

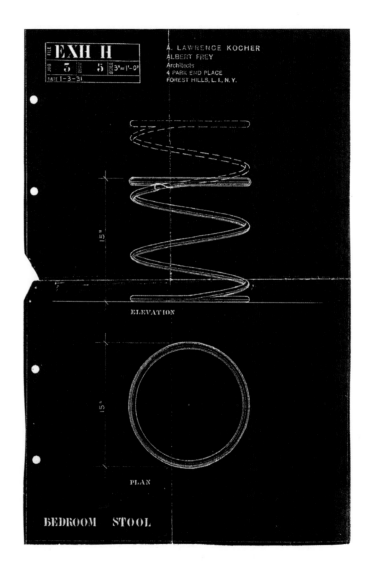

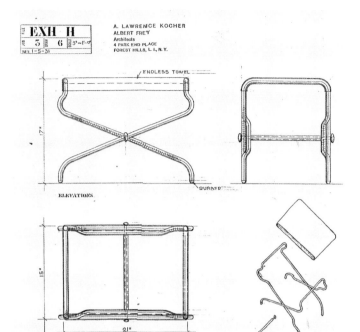

ENDLESS TOWEL

ELEVATIONS

RUBBED

PLAN

BATHROOM STOOL

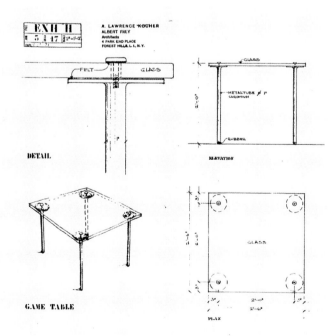

FELT GLASS

METAL TUBE ∅ 1"
CHROMIUM

GLASS

RUBBER

DETAIL

ELEVATION

GLASS

PLAN

GAME TABLE

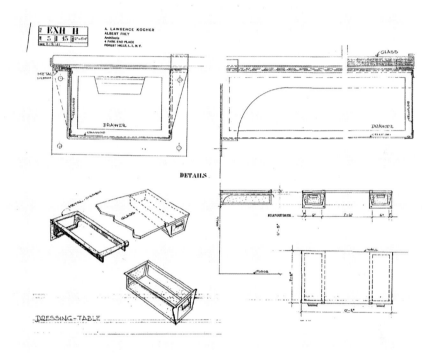

METAL
CHROMIUM

DRAWER

GLASS

DETAILS

DRAWER

ELEVATIONS

WALL

FLOOR

DRESSING-TABLE

OPPOSITE

LEFT: Figure 1.35 Inflatable rubber chairs. Ties hold the form, similar to English leather Chesterfields. Albert Frey drawing, December 3, 1930.

RIGHT: Figure 1.36 Bedroom stool. Albert Frey drawing, January 3, 1931.

UPPER LEFT: Figure 1.37 Bathroom stool with "endless towel." Albert Frey drawing, January 5, 1931.

LEFT: Figure 1.38 Glass game table. Albert Frey drawing, February 3, 1931.

RIGHT: Figure 1.39 Dressing table. Albert Frey drawing, February 2, 1931.

ANALYSIS OF THE HOUSE

An analysis of any architecture breaks the complex structure down to its essential features. The analysis of the Aluminaire House will deal with the formal and spatial order of the building and the circulation that reveals it (see fig. 1.42 on page 41).

The house is elementally based on a cubic form with voids carved into it (see fig. 1.42, diagram 1). It follows a Le Corbusier diagram of 1929 that describes four composition types, one of which is a carved cubic *parti*, represented by the Villa Savoye at Poissy, a project that Albert Frey worked on in Le Corbusier's office (see figs. 1.40, 1.45, and 1.46). The distortion of a pure cube (22 feet 6 inches x 28 feet 9 inches x 27 feet 3 inches) in the Aluminaire House expresses the one-way cantilever system, as was typical in Le Corbusier's work. The three aluminum columns (piloti) on each side of the house establish a center space on the long axis (viewed from the front), with no center on the short axis (see diagram 3). The plan utilizes this column grid to divide the house into front and back segments using wall units and the stairs (see diagrams 5 & 6).

The front areas of the house (toward the entry) that contain the two terraces and the bedroom are oriented toward the front façade, while the spaces behind on each level—the garage, living and dining rooms, and library—have their primary orientation toward the side façade (see diagrams 4 & 10). This rotation is reinforced by the circulation of the stair switching between zones. The vertical circulation in the center requires that one go around the center to continue up or down. It also pushes circulation horizontally to the periphery between the front and back zones to the cantilevered zones outside the columns on each floor (see diagram 6). This sense of dynamic movement from center to edge is reinforced by the diagonal solid parapets, which also alternate on sides of the center wall as the stairs go up through the floors (see diagram 5).

TOP: **Figure 1.40** "Four Building Types," Le Corbusier.

BOTTOM: **Figure 1.41** Axonometric of the structure of the house as built. Drawing by Frances Campani.

Each level of the house has an L-shaped plan of principal spaces, and in each case the L has a different orientation from the previous floor (see diagram 7). This further reinforces the rotation. On the ground floor entry, the curve of the foyer and semicircle of the boiler enclosure form an L space (see diagram 7). On the second level, there are two possible L-shape configurations: the living/dining/ kitchen areas identifying the public areas, or the dining/living/bedroom spaces denoting the principal living areas, leaving the kitchen/ bathroom as a utility block (see diagram 8). An L-shape volume is also created by the double height of the living and dining space (see diagram 8). On the upper floor, an L shape is created with the library in one quadrant and the terrace in the other two is formed with the third-level library and the double-height living room on the second level (see diagram 9). A final L-shape is formed on the roof as the solid roof cuts out over the terrace with the open lawn (see diagram 9).

This notion of rotation is yet again reinforced with the horizontal strip window on the front façade juxtaposed to the vertical orientation of the garage door and double-height window on the side façade. The oblique "preferred" view of the house focuses on this

reading. The two dominant and competing façades, the front and the side, also form an L, creating a horizontal/vertical tension (see diagram 10). The double-height living room with its massive window is the central focus of the house and its strongest space visually. At seventeen feet high by twelve feet by fifteen feet, the living room is activated visually by the exposed aluminum columns and beam structure, the vertical hovering shaft of the shower, and the stair with its solid parapet from the entry below to the library above (see fig. 1.18). In its original condition, the form of the shower on two chrome pipes holding the combined glass cabinet and dining table acted as a sculptural centerpiece around which the space flowed.

The front façade of the Aluminaire House is divided into horizontal bands, with the continuous window array in the center of the whole façade. The entry level is an open eight-foot space; the second level offers a solid four-foot wall topped by a five-foot-tall band of windows. The third level completes the composition with a four-foot parapet, five feet of open space, and a small one-foot, three-inch band at the roofline (see diagram 11). The bottom open space is larger than those above, making the solid façade seem to float.

The second-level window mullions create an operable section in the center (two and a half feet tall), flanked top and bottom by one-foot, three-inch window sections. These window divisions create an interesting rhythm on the façade (see diagram 15), and present the reading of the front façade as a dominant solid center, flanked top and bottom by narrower voids.

The vertical window mullion pattern reveals the vertical girt spacing of 3 foot 8 ½ inches, which forms six equal bays (see diagram 16). A counterpoint is created by the exposed columns at the bottom and top terraces (visible through the middle band of windows) forming an alternate rhythm of narrow sides and wide middle spaces. The bay divisions create a stabilizing repetitive order against which the column grid and horizontal matrix play. The aluminum panels that overlap on the top and right-hand side form a subtle grid (3 foot 8 ½ inches wide by 4 foot high) over the whole that, like the windows, corresponds to the underlying girt spacing. This pattern is further embellished by the screws of the panels, which generate an off-center or tartan grid, creating a subtle visual syncopation.

The back façade is entirely solid, and here the tartan grid of panels and screws provides simple visual elegance and scale (see diagram 16). This façade was visible in the exhibition and a door with stairs was cut into it to facilitate circulation.[23] This façade could have had windows for the living and dining rooms or library above, so its blankness can only be explained that two units were expected to be joined together, as were the Loucheur houses that Frey had worked on in Le Corbusier's office (see figs. 1.47 and 1.48). This is also a common American type of home for low-rise, high-density neighborhoods on the edge of cities that would permit the complex community patterns, like Forest Hills Queens, that Kocher and Frey were advocating at the time of the exhibition (see Chapter 2).

If the front and back façades establish the system and its gridded complexity, the side façades play a different strategy of cutout solids and voids of nearly equal sizes (see diagrams 13 & 14). While the front and back façades are simple and symmetrical, the sides are dynamic and have no central dominant figure. The cutouts go to the edges of the façades, and the remaining surface areas are of differing sizes and shapes. The solid/void compositions of the two side façades are enlivened by the windows, girt, panel, and screw patterns that also relate them to the front and back façades. The aluminum panels become a Cartesian grid of horizontals and verticals activated by the cutouts—a fundamentally Corbusian idea.

The Aluminaire House possesses no apparent proportioning system or geometric regulating lines. Instead, the form of the house and its solids and voids seem to be regulated by the materials. There is a distinct avoidance of exact squares throughout the composition, indicating that the joining and lapping of the parts express how the house was to be put together.

OPPOSITE

Figure 1.42 Analytic diagrams of the form of the house.

1 Cubic form.

2 Structural grid—5-inch aluminum columns define space.

3 Local symmetries—single symmetry at front and back and double at sides.

4 Rotated axis—front space faces forward while back space faces sideways.

5 Shear walls—two walls sandwich the diagonal stair.

6 Shear planes and diagonal planes—horizontal (floor) planes are cut away to create vertical spatial relationships.

7 Dining-living vertical volumetric L's. Public vertical volumetric L of kitchen, dining, and vertical living room and the private horizontal volumetric L of the bedroom, exercise area, and bathroom.

8 Living-dining vertical L and bedroom-bathroom L.

9 Horizontal front façade and vertical side façade.

10 Façades—horizontal front/vertical side.

11–12 Façades—front and back are simple, regular form.

13–14 Façades—side façades are dynamic irregular forms.

15–16 Façade grids—syncopated tartan of windows, panels, and screws.

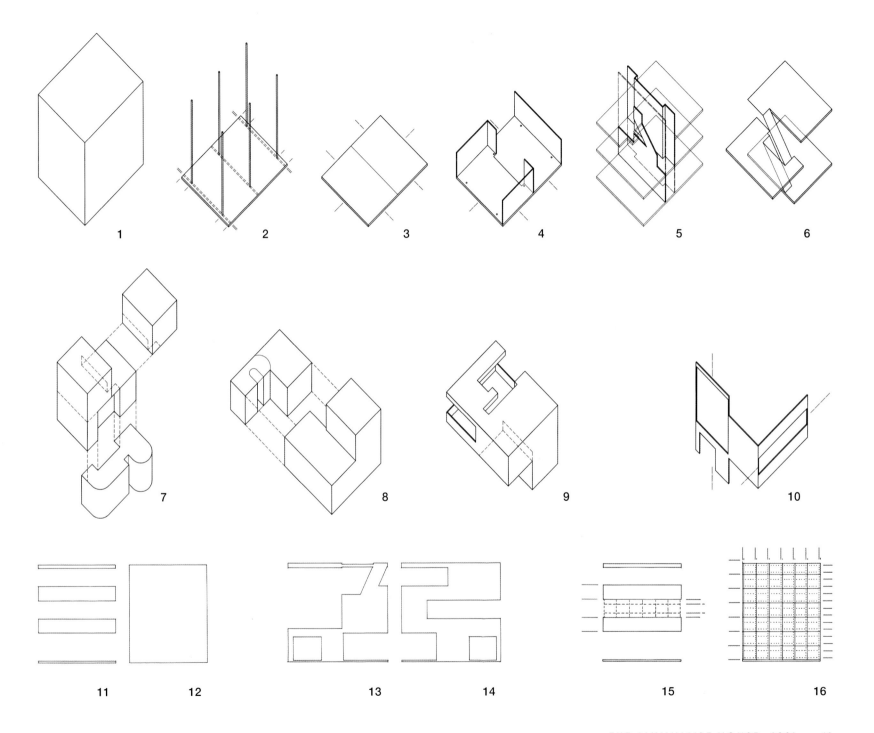

1   2   3   4   5   6

7   8   9   10

11   12   13   14   15   16

THE ARCHITECTS

Figure 1.43 A. Lawrence Kocher, Black Mountain School, circa 1940.

ALFRED LAWRENCE KOCHER was an architect, educator, author, and editor.[24] He was born in San Jose, California, in 1885 and died in Williamsburg, Virginia, in 1969. Kocher received his BA from Stanford University in 1903. He studied at MIT from 1910 to 1912, and Pennsylvania State College from 1912 to 1916 where he received his MA while also working as an instructor. He became a full professor at Penn State in 1918, started the degree program in architecture, and served as head of the department. From 1926 to 1928 he was head of the School of Architecture at the University of Virginia. From 1928 to 1940 Kocher was a visiting professor at the Carnegie Institute of Technology. In 1940 he taught at the avant-garde Black Mountain College in North Carolina. From 1944 to 1959 he was Lecturer in the Fine Arts at the College of William and Mary in Williamsburg.

Kocher's professional interests were diverse. From 1928 to 1954 he was a member of the advisory committee for architecture for the restoration of Williamsburg. Kocher was appointed editor of the *Architectural Records* of Colonial Williamsburg in 1944. According to his *New York Times* obituary of June 8, 1969,[25] Kocher was an early member of the International Congress of Modern Architects (CIAM), an international group of architects interested in the modern city that met from 1928 to 1959 and was heavily influenced by Le Corbusier.

Kocher was also a writer. He published a twelve-part article, "Early Architecture of Pennsylvania," for *Architectural Record* in 1920–21, as well as a two-part "American Country House" in 1925–26. He became associate editor at *Architectural Record* in 1927 and managing editor from 1928 to 1938. The magazine announced that "it was embarking on a new chapter in its history . . . from a beaux-arts periodical into one espousing a broad concept of modern architecture."[26]

At the very time when modernism reached America, Kocher had contact with contemporary criticism and with manufacturers of building products and components—those industries on which his magazine would have relied on financially for advertising income. It was through these professional contacts that Kocher met Walter T. Sweatt, codirector of the Architectural League and Allied Arts Exhibition, whose request gave rise to the Aluminaire House.

Kocher also practiced architecture, although he never established a commercial practice. He was one of the few Americans interested in modernism before 1930. He partnered with architect Gerhard Zeigler in 1929 to design the Sunlight Towers, a hypothetical project for New York, and in 1930 on a house for author Rex Stout in Fairfield County, Connecticut. For the 1929 Architectural League exhibition, Kocher and Zeigler designed a display booth of an "architect's office with furniture" for F. W. Dodge Corp. Zeigler returned to Europe in 1930, leaving an opening for Albert Frey.

ALBERT FREY was born on October 13, 1903, in Zurich, Switzerland, to an upper middle-class family that was educated and involved in the arts.[27] Frey seemed to have both a natural gift and an enormous enthusiasm for making things and for putting materials together. As a child, he fashioned canoes out of wood and canvas. His first use of aluminum was in making toys for his young sister out of discarded aluminum soap cans.[28]

Frey attended the Institute of Technology, Technikum, in Winterthur, Switzerland, receiving a technical education with a diploma in 1924. After graduating he traveled to Italy, and then moved to Brussels to work for Jean-Jules Eggericx and Raphael Verwilghen from 1925 to 1927. He worked on detailing buildings already in construction. In 1928 Frey was back in Switzerland and worked for Levenberger/Fluckiger, detailing and producing construction drawings. During this time, Frey designed a "Minimal Metal House" of about 720 square feet with three bedrooms (with drawings in Le Corbusier style).

Figure 1.44 Albert Frey on the Aluminaire House roof terrace.

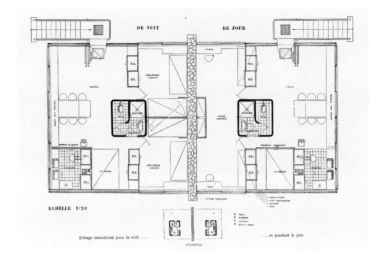

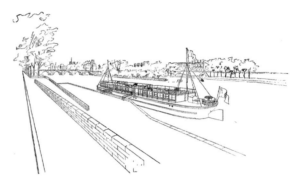

LEFT

TOP: Figure 1.45 Villa Savoye at Poissy, France, Le Corbusier, 1929–1933.

CENTER:Figure 1.46 Villa Savoye roof terrace drawing by Le Corbusier. This cubic house carves outdoor space into volumes as does the Aluminaire House.

BOTTOM:Figure 1.47 Maison Loucheur, perspective, Le Corbusier, 1929.

ABOVE

TOP: Figure 1.48 Maison Loucheur, night and day plans. An economy of space.

BOTTOM:Figure 1.49 Asile Flottant de l'Armée du Salut (Salvation Army residence). Le Corbusier, 1929.

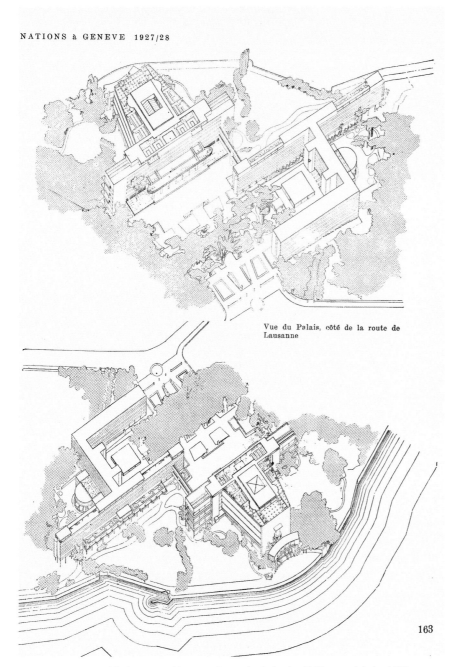

Vue du Palais, côté de la route de Lausanne

163

Figure 1.50 League of Nations competition entry, Geneva. Le Corbusier, 1927; second design 1929.

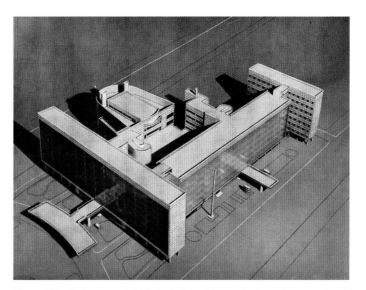

Figure 1.51 Centrosoyuz administrative building, Moscow. Le Corbusier, 1928–1933.

Frey went to Paris and worked for Le Corbusier from October 1928 to July 1929. He was one of two paid, full-time employees. Charlotte Perriand, Jose Luis Sert, and Kunio Maekawa also worked in the office. Although many of Le Corbusier projects were in the works at the time, including the Villa Savoye (see figs. 1.45 and 1.46), Villa Church and Ville d'Avray, Cite de Refuge and the Asile Flottant (see fig. 1.49), the League of Nations competition (second submission, fig. 1.50), the Centrosoyuz administration building in Moscow (see fig. 1.51), the Mundaneum project for Geneva, and the Prager factory project. The Maisons Loucheur (figs. 1.47 and 1.48) is the only project that Frey was able to work on with Le Corbusier in its design phase.[29] During his time in Le Corbusier's office Frey talked of his desire to work in the United States, where new materials were available for use in construction. He also applied for a visa to visit the United States.

Frey went back to work for Eggericx and Verwilghen, but soon received his visa for the United States. He arrived in New York on September 5, 1930. He looked for work at the office of the Swiss immigrant William Lescaze, Philip Goodwin, and A. Lawrence Kocher. Kocher responded first, and not only hired Frey but gave him a place to live in his house and studio in Forest Hills, Queens. Kocher's work on the Rex Stout house and the Sunlight Towers may have been what attracted Frey to his office.

By all indications Albert Frey was responsible for the formal design of the Aluminaire House and its repeatable variations, while we might attribute the program for the project to Lawrence Kocher. When Kocher responded to Sweatt in 1930 to make something for the 1931 Allied Arts and Industries exhibition,[30] he quickly brought Frey on board. The freestanding exhibition house was proposed, and the design completed in seven months. It was constructed in ten days for the April 1931 opening.

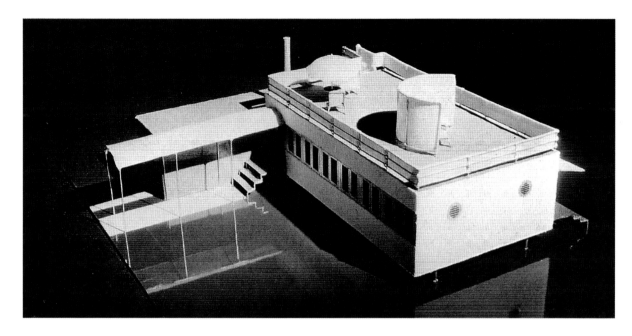

OPPOSITE

LEFT: Figure 1.52 Farmhouse A model, 1931.

RIGHT: Figure 1.53 Farmhouse B model, 1931.

Figure 1.54 Experimental five-room house,
Cotton Textile Industry, study model and plan, 1932.

While working with Kocher on the Aluminaire House, Frey also was involved in two versions of a prototype metal farmhouse—A and B—for the Committee of Farmhouse Design of the Presidents Conference on Home Building and Home Ownership, of which Kocher was a member (see figs. 1.52 and 1.53). From July 1931 to July 1932, Frey also worked part-time for William Lescaze. Work in Lescaze's office included the Chrystie-Forsyth Street Housing development (see fig. 2.12) and studies for the Museum of Modern Art.

In 1932, Frey worked with Kocher on the Experimental Weekend House and the Experimental Five Room House for the Cotton Textile Institute (see figs. 1.54, 1.55, and 1.56). This work was extended to the design of the Kocher Canvas Weekend House—built in 1934 and lasting until the 1950s (see figs. 1.57 and 1.58).

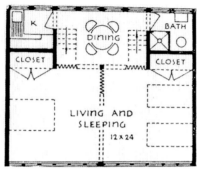

LEFT: **Figure 1.55** Experimental weekend house, Cotton Textile Industry, study model and plan, 1932.

RIGHT: **Figure 1.56** Experimental weekend house plan, 1932.

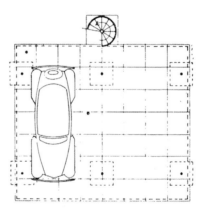
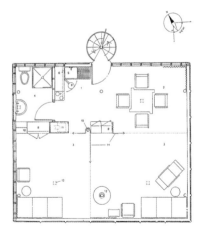

LEFT: **Figure 1.57** Kocher canvas weekend house, 1934.

RIGHT: **Figure 1.58** Kocher house plans.

In October 1934, Albert Frey left for Palm Springs, California, to work on the Kocher-Samson Building (see fig. 5.13). He returned to New York briefly from 1937 to 1939 to work with Philip Goodwin while the Museum of Modern Art was under construction. During this time he also did some work with Kocher, and wrote and published a book, *In Search of a Living Architecture*.[31] Frey left New York in July of 1939 to settle permanently in Palm Springs.

The partnership of Kocher and Frey was a potent combination, though relatively short-lived. Work was scarce during the depression. Kocher went on to teach at Black Mountain School in North Carolina while Frey stayed in the western desert and mountains, where he had a long and productive career in Palm Springs, California. He never lost his enthusiasm for the inventive use of materials, or for modernism, but his work evolved formally in response to the desert landscape and climate (see Chapter 5).

Figure 1.59 Albert Frey and Lawrence Kocher, lunch at Rockefeller Cafeteria, New York, 1931.

2

CONTEXT AND ISSUES

THE DEBATE OF PREFABRICATION VERSUS COMMUNITY

In January and February 1930, *Architectural Record* published an article in two parts by Lewis Mumford titled "Mass-Production and the Modern House."[1] Lawrence Kocher, managing editor at *Record*, certainly must have been very familiar with the article. In fact, the Aluminaire House project seemed to answer Mumford's concerns and warnings about contemporary mass production of houses.

Mumford's long and sobering article was both resigned and cautionary. In the January issue, Mumford described prefabrication in construction as a transformation already achieved—and of enormous importance to contemporary architecture.

> *During the last hundred and fifty years a great change has taken place in architecture. This change has nothing to do with the superficial esthetics that agitated the architectural world: the quarrels between the classicists and the medievalists or between the traditionalists and the modernists are all meaningless in terms of it. I refer to the process whereby manufacture has step by step taken the place of the art of building, and all the minor processes of construction have shifted from the job itself to the factory.*

Mumford pointed out, without condemnation, the profession's reliance on Sweet's Catalog, but he bemoaned the fact that the change had occurred without any revolution in design, and that even the cost reductions were limited. He observed that the changes in building methods had not altered the forms of building and that the assembly of parts taking place on the building site attempted to mimic the "art of building" that it replaced. (Kocher may have asked Frey to design the Aluminaire precisely in order to turn this notion around, as the parts and the joinery *are* the aesthetic elements of the Aluminaire House.)

Mumford, however, saw further shortcomings in the mass production of housing. One, he claimed, was the necessity for continuous turnover, which made less sense for housing than for shorter-lived products. Another complaint was the limited cost savings of mass production on the final cost of a house—land and infrastructure being of more significance. He remained dubious about the actual benefits of mass production, which he insisted counted for much of the process already. Most importantly, he saw the community as the primary contemporary concern, and he devoted the second part of the article to this. He concluded his first article as follows:

> *Is there perhaps a more radical approach to the problem of housing than the engineer and the mechanically minded architect have conceived? I think there is; for though Mr. (Buckminster) Fuller, for example, believes that he has swept aside all traditional tags in dealing with the house, and has faced its design with inexorable rigor, he has kept, with charming unconsciousness, the most traditional tag of all, namely, the freestanding individual house. If we are thorough enough in our thinking to throw that prejudice aside too, we may, I suspect still find a place for the architect in modern civilization.*

Along with the concept of the honest aesthetic of standardized parts, Kocher and Frey insisted on the concept of the community of units[2] (see fig. 2.1). Le Corbusier's Esprit Nouveau Pavilion in the Exposition Internationale in Paris 1925, an exhibition house and repeatable unit, was probably a conceptual precedent for Frey, and seems to have influenced him formally as well (see figs. 2.29 and 2.32). The unit configurations advanced by Kocher and Frey in 1931 also might have been a response to Mumford's article. The tone of "Mass-Production and the Modern House" was critical of the then-current enthusiasm for mass production which Mumford saw as ignoring the issues of community planning while being caught up in the excitement for a "new and improved" house as a product. Kocher was not given the task of making the Aluminaire House a product, he was given the task of selling products, and in making this unit, he may have wanted to address Mumford's critique. In their article on lot development in *Architectural Record*, April 1931, Kocher and Frey depicted the Aluminaire House as a repeatable, attached unit forming a community (see figs. 2.2 and 2.3).

The second part of "Mass-Production and the Modern House" continued Mumford's argument that not only was the freestanding house romantic nonsense, but wrong-headed in the most basic way. He pointed out the existing reality of the linkage of dwellings through services (water, sewer, electricity), and thus the fiction of the independent house. He concluded that the community *was* the unit. Kocher and Frey's "Real Estate Subdivisions for Low Cost Housing" addressed this issue head on, applying the "superblock" concept utilized by Henry Wright and Clarence Stein at the Sunnyside Gardens project that Mumford admired (see fig. 2.21).

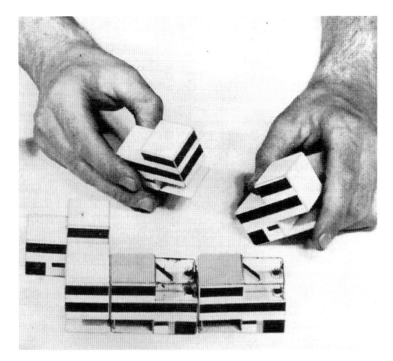

Figure 2.1 Albert Frey, playing with housing units.

At the time of the 1931 Architectural League exhibition, the weekly *New Republic* included an article on architecture every second or third week. These were often by Douglas Haskell, who also wrote for the *Nation* during this period. It was Catherine Bauer, however, who covered the Architectural League exhibition in *The New Republic*, in a review that was quite critical of the show. Haskell wrote a much longer, and even less enthusiastic, piece for *Parnassus*, which is perhaps why he stepped out of his usual role at *The New Republic*.[3] In these simultaneous reviews, both Bauer and Haskell pointed to the Aluminaire House as the only breath of fresh air in the otherwise very conservative League exhibition. Bauer wrote:

One, and only one, exhibit displays any curiosity whatsoever about the modern possibilities in a type solution for small dwellings. This is Mr. Kocher's aluminum house, built full-size from standard materials, completely and economically functional. It is a fine and stimulating piece of work and well worth the seventy-five-cent admission and even the general chaos.[4]

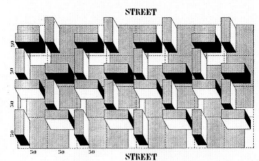

STREET

50 | 50 | 50 | 50 | 50

STREET

Improved subdivision with same area and number of houses shown on opposite page:

(Black indicates blank walls.)
Houses are wide and shallow.
Broad garden area is at side of house.
All windows are at side toward garden.
There is attractiveness and individuality in grouping.

There is unobstructed sunlight and privacy because of wide spacing and staggered arrangement.
Garage included in cube of house.
One driveway serves four houses with minimum encroachment on garden area.

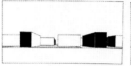

Front view showing wide and open spacing on plots 50' x 50'.

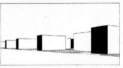

Elimination of monotony by "staggered" arrangement. Houses on street are 100' on centers.

The houses illustrated at right, in Forest Hills Gardens, Long Island, Wilson Eyre, architect, are made attractive by their staggered grouping.

The real estate subdivision with low-cost houses may be given a similar setting by arrangement suggested on this page. The entire block may be treated as a garden.

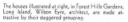

An actual example of scheme proposed above.

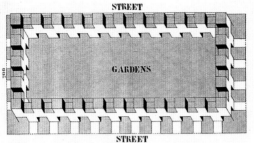

STREET

GARDENS

STREET

Continuous houses. Where land values are excessive and recreation areas are nearby it is logical to accept the continuous arrangement. Open porches on the ground floor penetrate the row and establish a relation between street and garden. Free passage of air is admitted to the garden court. Each house is provided with a roof terrace overlooking the garden.

P ROOM
E ENTRANCE
G GARAGE
L LAUNDRY
H HEATER

S STORAGE
HA HALL
L R LIVING ROOM
D R DINING ROOM
K KITCHEN

B R BED ROOM
B BATH
C CLOSET
T TERRACE

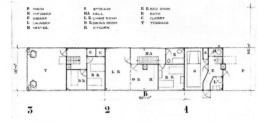

3   **2**   **4**

Proposed floor arrangement for above scheme.

Typical and undesirable continuous houses showing pretentious (false) fronts and a depressing side toward the court.

The housing scheme on opposite page is intended for the small lot subdivisions that exist where land values are high. The characteristic feature of this house scheme proposed is the location of ground porch and roof terrace at opposite ends. This makes it possible to obtain, simultaneously, sunshine or shade. When placed in rows as single houses the position of terrace and porch alternates, giving privacy between blank walls of neighboring houses. Windows of living and sleeping rooms face to front and rear. The area occupied by the house is regained for outdoor living space by roof garden and inside porch.

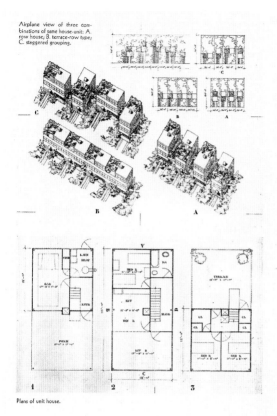

Airplane view of three combinations of same house-unit: A. row house; B. terrace-row type; C. staggered grouping.

Plans of unit house.

4   **2**   **3**

Of course, if the League committee had had anything to say about it, the Aluminaire House would almost certainly not have been in the exhibition—it was a commercial products display, as Haskell pointed out in *Parnassus*.

Mr. Kocher's full-scale aluminum house, curiously enough, was not sponsored by the committee but was a "commercial" exhibit sponsored by manufacturers and contractors. That, too, was indicative; for the motor of present events seems to be industrial change.[5]

OPPOSITE

FAR LEFT, FIRST IMAGE: Figure 2.2 *Architectural Record*, April 1931.

OPPOSITE AND ABOVE

Figure 2.3 Kocher and Frey's article on housing.

THE REJECTED ARCHITECTS EXHIBITION

Architect Philip Johnson's 1931 exhibition, also known as the "Refused Architects," was organized in response to the Architectural League jury selections, which essentially excluded anything that smacked of European modernism. Douglas Haskell and Catherine Bauer both discussed in their respective newspaper articles the 1931 League exhibit in relation to the concurrent "Rejected Architects" exhibition on Seventh Avenue. Haskell praised the move to break away from the "dinosaurian exhibit of the New York Architectural League." He did not have much praise for Johnson's show itself, however. "In form, a great deal of the 'rejected' work consisted mainly of mutations of the box, piled up off-center."[6]

Bauer was much more positive about the alternate show, but she was looking for an urban program that the architects themselves had not proposed. She wrote of the show:

> The most striking thing about these models and photographs is that the designers have apparently no distinguishing or competitive tricks. Some are without doubt more competent than others—but as the eye roves over the exhibits, one does not stop to exclaim. Instead one goes on—visualizes whole communities, whole cities made up of buildings like these, each bearing an orderly relation to the others, each perfectly and wastelessly functional in itself. One is perhaps disappointed to find no large plan on the walls to facilitate such activity, but there can be little doubt that these architects have such plans in their minds.[7]

Haskell also had objections to the house as aesthetically "crude," but was supportive of it as an "idea." His reading of the idea, however, was not identical to the one put forward by Kocher and Frey.

The next issue of the *The New Republic* (following Bauer's review) was May 13, 1931, and Haskell's architectural entry, "The House of the Future," was a call to exploit mass production in order to update the building industry.[8] Haskell expressed disgust with the slow progress in building methods and suggested an entrepreneur should revolutionize the process. He cited the automobile industry as a model. He pursued the demand for a better "product," and also described the financial methods of acquiring this product.

> At a glance the intelligent reader will realize that the factory built house, or multiple-family dwelling, can be financed as cars and radios are, with an enormous expansion of credit, and an increased independence of the land. When housing finally follows our other industries out of its present handicraft, special-instance stage into an industrial one, we shall have twice as good a house for half what it costs today.

Three weeks after the appearance of "The House of the Future," *The New Republic* gave space to Lewis Mumford for a detailed response in "The Flaw in the Mechanical House."[9] Here Mumford described the shortcomings, and indeed dangers, of simply encouraging competitive efficiency in the industry. He raised specific objections to Haskell's claims on the economy of such a project.

In short, no decent "house of the future" can be designed in the factory alone. To forget this is to foster specious hopes; and if the mechanized house is placed on the market before appropriate community and regional plans are made for it, the result will be the same drab, inefficient and nasty environment that the speculative builder creates today. A high total efficiency in the mechanized house, without modern community planning, is a myth. There are one or two other little points . . . the possibilities of overproduction, competitive stylization, premature obsolescence—possibilities that are now notorious in the automobile and plumbing industries—[that] must be canvassed in any discussion of the factory-made house. We need . . . not merely community and regional plans; we also need social control of the means of production, and a regulation of output and prices in terms of the needs that are to be served and the human ends that are to be accomplished. This takes us closer to Ernst May in Frankfort than it does to Mr. Ford and his ingenious but overrated Model-T. A communism of technique in the production of houses, with the usual anarchy and monopoly in our system of land-holding, financing and community design, is an unworkable anachronism. No one who accepts this situation as inevitable has considered all the implications of the house of the future: for if our basic institutions and ideals are not changed, the more the house is altered, the more it will remain the same.

Haskell and Mumford exchanged one more round in the *The New Republic* (July 1 and 8, 1931, respectively). Haskell accused Mumford of dragging his feet—of objecting to progress. Mumford accused Haskell of not recognizing an ally when he saw one.[10]

The Aluminaire House, nominally an eye-catching display for building products, embodied important aspects of housing as an issue in modern architecture. For Kocher and Frey, these issues were intentional.

Rising to the challenge presented by Mumford in "Mass-Production and the Modern House," Kocher and Frey offered an architectural solution to Mumford's valid, but formless, suggestion. However, both Haskell and Mumford missed the more complex point about the Aluminaire House in their 1931 exchange. Had the house and its urban configurations for low-cost housing been physically attached to the house in the exhibition, as was the case with Le Corbusier's Esprit Nouveau Pavilion of 1925, they might have seen the idea in its totality, and both championed the project.

One thing seems certain about the Aluminaire Exhibition House of 1931: it pointed to two decisive departures from the status quo in architectural practice of the time. One, it used standard, available materials, suggesting the possibility of mass production. Two, it represented a repeatable unit, the configurations of which were proposed publicly by the architects. The Aluminaire House also "looked different," but this fact was also passed over in the debate it seems to have instigated in 1931.

THE ALUMINAIRE HOUSE AS MODERN ARCHITECTURE

The early period of the modern movement in architecture staunchly professed not to be a "style." It argued for a break with the styles that preceded it by proclaiming to be style-less. Mies van der Rohe stated this position directly in 1923: "We refuse to recognize problems of form, but only problems of building. Form is not the aim of our work, but only the result. Form, by itself, does not exist. Form as an aim is formalism; and that we reject."[11]

These common pronouncements against style and form, or "formalism," were a reaction to the Beaux Arts system of education that centered on classical, formal composition. Modern architecture's theory proposed that to achieve a radical break with the existing visual and social conditions, which reflected a conservative reliance on tradition and the past, the new architecture had to be derived from concerns for function and construction. These were deemed appropriate because the social, economic, political, and cultural conditions of the modern present, the "spirit of the age," or zeitgeist, demanded it. Mies van der Rohe summed up these three polemical concerns of function, construction, and zeitgeist timeliness

when he pronounced, "Architecture is the will of the epoch translated into space: living, changing, new. Not yesterday, not tomorrow, only today can be given form. Only this kind of building will be creative. Create form out of the nature of our tasks with the methods of our time. This is our task."[12]

The Aluminaire House, born out of a request to show construction with new materials, was a product of this thought and was derived from these intentions. It claimed to be a "house for contemporary living" and embodied these most important issues of the modern movement.

The new architecture was to be of and about its time. Mies states poetically, "The new era is a fact, it exists regardless of our 'yes' or 'no.' Yet it is neither better nor worse than any other era. It is a pure 'datum,' in itself without value or content. We reject all aesthetic speculation, all doctrine, all formalism."[13]

The modern artists' and architects' conception of the zeitgeist was formed and defined by their alliance with progressive social and political movements of the late nineteenth and early twentieth centuries.

These movements responded to the needs and demands brought about by the Industrial Revolution. As a consequence, most European governments explored political theories of egalitarianism in the early twentieth century. New social and cultural movements came with progressive politics, and modern architects chose to address what they saw as the specific needs of contemporary society. This was the rationale for the functionalist and constructional theories that replaced the earlier formal theory. The concerns for function and construction were believed to be a natural expression, beyond the narrow role given by style. The decision to build the Aluminaire House as a modern affordable house was clearly generated by a belief in the same zeitgeist.

The concerns for construction and structural systems were considered rational approaches to design through scientific understanding of the materials. Again, Mies stated, "Essentially our task is to free the practice of building from the control of aesthetic speculators and restore it to what it should exclusively be: building."[14] The authors of the Aluminaire House followed this same attitude toward construction and building. The idea to design and display the whole system for the construction of the building went far beyond the need to display new products.

The industrial process and the machine were also products of modern science and engineering. New methods of construction utilizing machine-made materials were manifested architecturally in European modernism. The industrialized process that created these materials was also of interest as a possible means for constructing factory-made buildings. The assembly-line process became applicable to prefabrication of architectural elements or of whole buildings, particularly housing. These ideas and actions had a clear effect on the conception of the

Aluminaire House. Revealing the logic of the structural system and expressing the assembly of machine prefabricated parts was stronger, in fact, than most of its European precedents.

Provoked by the modern study of "social science," functionalism, as it was soon called, became the concept of developing building plans from a concern for the relationships of the activities and uses of space. The function of a building should generate design ideas. A rational, if not scientific, organization of human actions should replace traditional modes of living. Efficiency of planning should reduce space within a house as well as save time and energy in domestic work (see fig. 2.7).

Although not solicited, the Aluminaire House for "contemporary living" sought to

evoke this concept as critical for the proper display of modern construction materials. The Aluminaire House followed the tenets of the Le Corbusier and Mies van der Rohe's notion of the "free plan"—the separation of function from the constraints of structure and enclosure. It is a literal representation of Le Corbusier's *Maison Dom-ino* in a metal frame—the Cartesian tableau on which to stage life's actions (see figs. 2.4 and 2.5).

However, the zeitgeist that interested the modern architect in Europe had both conservative and liberal forces at work. By the early 1930s, opposing political forces had prevailed and modern architecture was left without a cause. Not only were the progressive forces suppressed, but there were also serious flaws in the concept that

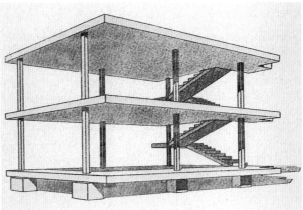

form could be derived solely from issues such as construction and function. The world of architecture soon came to understand that structure, construction, and function are sources that provide information and criteria, or serve as critical tests for making form or formal organizations but are not form generators. Thus construction and function, inspired by an enthusiasm for progressive ideology, became the agents for developing the new style, not avoiding it. Le Corbusier noted, "Style is a unity of principle animating all the work of an epoch, the result of a state of mind which has its own special character. Our own epoch is determining, day by day, its own style."[15]

However, the issue of whether early modernism was a style should not obscure its intentions that obviously affected its form. Today, one can argue that modern architecture was a style that sought to emphasize function and construction and the *zeitgeist* of "modern progressive life," but was expressed in the forms and aesthetics to distinguish itself. By the 1930s, encyclopedic books of modern architecture, such as Alberto Sartoris' *Architettura Funzionale*[16] or F.R.S. Yorke's *The Modern House*,[17] demonstrated that modern architecture was establishing itself throughout the world. It became commonplace to illustrate the visual coherence rather than discuss scientific issues of construction and function in modern society.

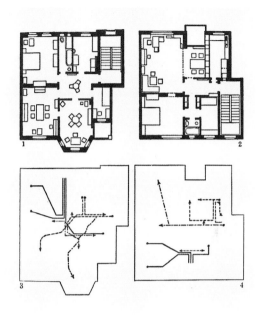

Figure 2.7 Circulation efficiency diagram, Karl Teige.

The need for change was not as urgent in America. The revolutionary spirit that dominated Europe at the turn of the century and challenged the traditionally rooted social, cultural, economic, and political structures was not as important a force in the United States, where these structures were still young, and the notion of economic growth outweighed any spirit of radical change. Colin Rowe made this distinction in "Chicago Frame" in his comparison of European and American architecture.[18] Here he acknowledged the invention of the high-rise steel skeleton frame in Chicago, while noting that its development occurred within "given" forms of American economic capitalist reality, as opposed to the European forms that reflected the theory of ideological change (see fig. 2.8).

It is for these reasons that modernism, when it did arrive in the United States, was not related to social issues such as public housing. It came depoliticized and was treated as an aesthetic option. From its American roots in Chicago through its transformed European "Bauhaus" education of the 1930s, modern architecture in the United States was favored for the bastions of capitalism, commerce, and finance, in the form of the skyscraper. The few American buildings that demonstrated a belief in the polemics of modern European architecture were primarily produced by expatriates. Rudolph Schindler's Pueblo Ribera Court Housing (1923) and Lovell beach house (1925–6), Richard Neutra's "Rush City Reformed" (1926–30) and Lovell house (1927–9), the Howe-Lescaze Philadelphia Savings Fund Society building (1928–32) and their Chrystie-Forsyth Street housing development (1931–33) are the principal examples (see figs. 2.9–2.13). Kocher was aware of and interested in this phenomenon through his two European partners, Gerhard Ziegler and Albert Frey. The Aluminaire House certainly fits into this expatriate camp and in fact was more overtly polemical than most of these works.

TOP: Figure 2.8 Skyscraper steel frame, Fair Store, Chicago, by William Le Baron Jenny, 1889–1890.

CENTER: Figure 2.9 Lovell Beach House, Rudolph Shindler, Los Angeles, California, 1925–1926.

BOTTOM: Figure 2.10 "Rush City Reformed," a plan for a model metropolis with a population of one million. Richard Neutra, 1926–1930.

UPPER LEFT: Figure 2.11 Lovell House, Richard Neutra, Los Angeles, California, 1927–1929.

LOWER LEFT: Figure 2.12 Chrystie-Forsyth Street housing, New York City, 1931–1933, Howe and Lescaze. Albert Frey worked on this project.

RIGHT: Figure 2.13 Philadelphia Savings Fund Society, Philadelphia, 1928–1932, Howe and Lescaze.

THE ALUMINAIRE HOUSE AS MODERN HOUSING

The Aluminaire House was conceived as a housing unit and looked to Europe for both social and architectural precedent. One of the significant aspects of the turn-of-the-century modern movement in Europe was its inextricable relationship to the issue of housing. Until this modern period, prominent architects built palaces, villas, mansions, or townhouses for wealthy patrons. The architects who founded the modern movement in Europe, however, developed "housing for the masses" for members of the emerging industrial working class who had migrated to the city in large numbers. Housing thus came to be seen for the first time as a new and important architectural problem. Housing for the proletariat as opposed to houses for the bourgeoisie, built by governments or institutions rather than for private clients, became a new pursuit. Other significant issues, such as standardization, mass production, and prefabrication were also pursued in direct relation to it.

The fundamental scheme and composition of the Aluminaire House comes from this European influence or precedent. The sociopolitical influence is evident in that a request to display building materials was executed through a model for repeatable affordable housing. The "House for Contemporary Living" in America was something that the working class could afford, in a rather dense urban neighborhood, and not a mansion on acres of private property. The rectilinear, abstract, simple forms and open planning clearly related to the housing built in Europe in the 1920s. Of course, European socialist ideas regarding subsidized housing had to be transformed into American capitalist notions regarding affordable housing.

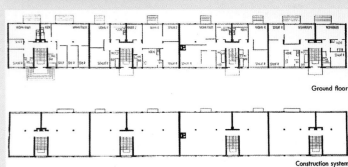

Ground floor

Construction system

Socialist theories were being applied by progressive governments in cities and regions throughout Europe at the turn of the century. The Weimar Republic in Germany, Syndicalisme in France, Fabianism in England, and other similar movements from Sweden, Holland, and Austria were concerned with the problems resulting from the Industrial Revolution. Low wages, poor health conditions, and a shortage of housing in cities brought architecture and social problems together. Progressive architects were interested in this linkage between social need and new theories for building. Housing the masses was the natural vehicle for such interests.

In Europe, individual architects and national cultures brought different issues to bear on the design of housing and its relationship to the social and physical context of the city. Many of the pioneers of the modern movement had significant involvement with housing within their careers. Le Corbusier's publication of his first work, *Oeuvre Complete 1910–29*, consisted of his important early houses as well as speculative housing projects and prototypes (see figs. 2.26–2.29). Mies van der Rohe's earliest work included the 1927 Weissenhof Siedlung project in Stuttgart, which entailed both the plan for the housing exhibition and its principal building (see figs. 2.14 and 2.15). Walter Gropius produced the housing for the city of Dessau while formulating the Bauhaus school in 1926, among several other housing projects in Germany, and designed a prefabricated unit at the Weissenhof Siedlung (see fig. 2.6). Other architects such as Mart Stam, Ernst May, Bruno Taut, Hugo Haring, Ludwig Hilbersheimer, and Otto Haessler of Germany, or J. J. P. Oud of Holland, worked almost exclusively with housing (see figs. 2.16, 2.17, and 2.22). Some significant architects like Berlage, Perret, May, Haessler, and Stam became public officials in socialist governments specifically to generate housing developments.

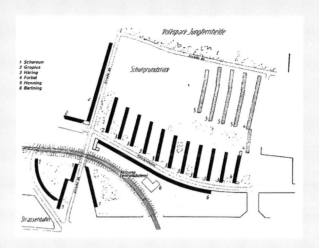

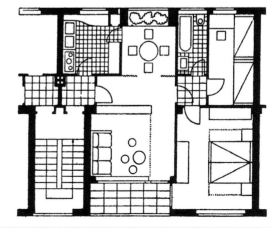

OPPOSITE

TOP: Figure 2.14 Weissenhof Siedlung housing exhibition, Stuttgart, Germany. Mies van der Rohe site plan, 1927.

MIDDLE AND BOTTOM: Figure 2.15 Apartment building at Weissenhof Seidlung, Mies van der Rohe, view and plan.

RIGHT

TOP: Figure 2.16 Siemensstat housing, Berlin, Germany, Hans Sharoun site plan, 1929.

MIDDLE AND BOTTOM: Figure 2.17 Apartment building at Siemensstat, Walter Gropius, view and plan.

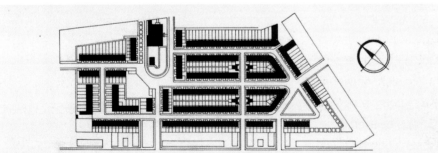

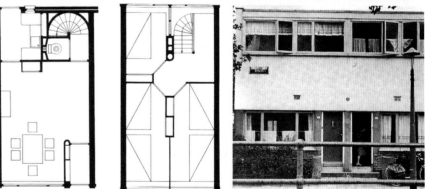

Figure 2.18 Kiefhook housing, Rotterdam, Netherlands, 1928, J. J. P. Oud, aerial view and site plan.

Figure 2.19 Kiefhook housing, Rotterdam, Netherlands, 1928, J. J. P. Oud, view and unit plan.

The Aluminaire House, particularly in its three- and four-bedroom versions published in *Architectural Record*, was influenced by the work in Europe. Efficiency studies led to careful condensed planning while housing codes established humanizing requirements for walk-up units with such criteria as floor-through units and balconies.

Its 1,100-square-foot compactness suggests that it was informed by the theory of "existence minimum," and its upper and lower terraces indicate comparable concerns for sunlight and air. The Aluminaire House, however, did not go to the extremes of function and efficiency practiced by the German architects, which led to thin building forms following a diagrammatic sun/air formula specifying orientation, height, and spacing (see figs. 2.20 and 2.24), which, when built in cities, disconnected the housing from any adjacent urban context. Instead the Aluminaire House opted for a configuration more in keeping with the housing in Holland, which fit into existing urban types and fabric. H. P. Berlage's Amsterdam South, for instance, is perimeter block housing that defines the public street with the interior of the block as common area for the residents (see fig. 2.22). J. J. P. Oud's Kiefhook housing in Rotterdam is also an example of successfully achieving this (see fig. 2.18). The 1931 *Architectural Record* article on housing by Kocher and Frey identifies the Aluminaire House as a "superblock" configuration and the blank façade of the Aluminaire House suggests joining two together, not unlike the Loucheur project that Frey worked on in Le Corbusier's office (see figs. 1.47 and 1.48).

The residential superblock scheme of the Aluminaire House could fit appropriately into a typical American urban grid. Kocher and Frey made a careful analysis of the neighborhood of Forest Hills, Queens, where they worked, and suggested similar patterns in which individual units could be interrelated to fit into existing conditions. This had already been done in nearby Sunnyside Gardens, Queens, by Clarence Stein and Henry Wright (see fig. 2.21). However, once free of the existing grid they were compelled to conform to in Queens, Stein and Wright moved to a different form of more suburban planning. The Aluminaire maintained a relation to the European model and was designed to be an urban solution rather than respond to the growing interest in suburban housing.

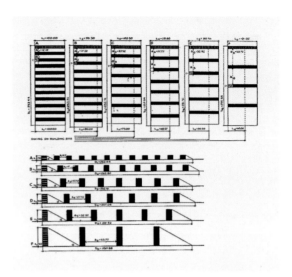

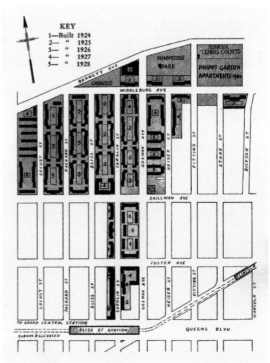

Accompanying the pursuit of the affordable dwelling, or mass housing in Europe, was the invention of, and experimentation with, prefabrication and mass production. The concept of the standardized unit implied a direct linkage to modern means of production. Construction systems were conceived to reduce the cost of housing. The house could be a "machine for living" made by a machine as had been done with so many other twentieth-century inventions—from the automobile to the washing machine. Two methods were explored: the prefabrication of parts to be assembled at the site, and the fabrication of whole units at the factory to be shipped complete to the site. Le Corbusier at Pessac, Gropius at Stuttgart (see fig. 2.6), and May in Frankfurt (see fig. 2.22) are the best known of those pursuing these possibilities. Albert Frey and Lawrence Kocher certainly knew these precedents, and the Aluminaire House was directly conceived in relation to them. In concert with America's competitive production of building materials and assemblies, the "off-the-shelf" nature of the Aluminaire House is one of the strongest attributes of its visual character.

In the United States, with the sophisticated development of mass production churning out varied building materials and the entrepreneurial spirit supported within the American culture, a tradition of prefabricated construction had already developed. While the country seemed skeptical of the new modern aesthetic, it displayed faith in technological progress. Standardized parts for construction were increasingly available in catalogs such as Sweet's. In the case of domestic architecture, however, there seemed to be an embarrassment about the new techniques, which appeared to many to represent a shortcut, or a poor substitute, for the real thing. In general, efforts were still made to make dwellings look conventionally built.

TOP: Figure 2.20 "Illustrating the Development of a Rectangular Building-Site with Parallel Rows of Tenement-Blocks of Different Heights" in relation to sun angles, Walter Gropius.

BOTTOM: Figure 2.21 Sunnyside Gardens, Queens, New York, superblocks, Clarence Stein and Henry Wright, 1924–1928.

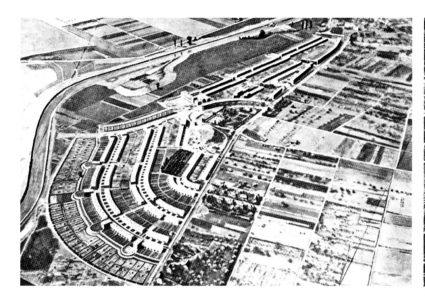

ABOVE LEFT: Figure 2.22 Romerstadt housing, Frankfurt, Germany, 1926–1928, Ernst May, Herbert Boehm, Wolfgang Bongert.

ABOVE RIGHT: Figure 2.23 Amsterdam Sud plan, 1914–1917, H. P. Berlage.

LEFT: Figure 2.24 Housing study of the "Existenzminimum" for Berlin, Germany, 1930, Ludwig Hilbersheimer.

EUROPEAN EXHIBITIONS

In Europe, the social and architectural interest in mass housing was demonstrated through housing exhibitions. Various cultural organizations provided assistance for experimental housing by sponsoring exhibitions. Foremost among these was the Deutscher Werkbund, founded in 1907 in Germany by artists in association with manufacturers, with varying aims ranging from craftsmanship to mass production. Similar organizations were formed in Austria, Switzerland, and England. The best known of these was the Werkbund exhibition in 1927, the Wiessenhof Siedlung in Stuttgart, in which Mies van der Rohe, vice president of the Werkbund, laid out a plan in which sixteen architects built twenty-one separate dwellings (see figs. 2.6, 2.14, 2.15, and 2.28). This was repeated in 1932 in Vienna by the Austrian Werkbund. These exhibitions attested to the commitment of progressive governments, social institutions, and modernist architects to housing. Lawrence Kocher, as an architectural editor, surely knew of these exhibitions, and Albert Frey visited the Wiessenhof Siedlung the year after it opened.

In America the focus of design attention was the individual unit rather than the community. With the banking mortgage system, the incredible growth of the automobile industry, and the birth of the parkway, the suburbanization of America became the predominant element of the American dream. The house was emphasized as a product to be on private property rather than owned by a city or town. However, within this atmosphere there were dissenting voices. Even before the economic crash of 1929, various American architects and planners addressed the shortcomings of this "individualistic" direction. Proponents for alternate block arrangements in New York were Andrew Thomas, George H. Wells, Horace Ginsbern, Springsteen and Goldhammer, and Wright and Stein.[19] Mumford argued for the design of communities in their entirety, as discussed in The Debate of Prefabrication versus Community, pages 52–58. The patronage for the early housing developments was mostly through labor unions or private philanthropic organizations. Government sponsorship of housing, which was occurring in Europe, was not present in the United States until Franklin D. Roosevelt's New Deal of 1932, and then it was geared to different architectural (and ultimately social) goals.

Though rational, the principles of modern architecture, particularly prefabrication, were not applied to urban housing in America. The Aluminaire House can be seen as an early voice, suggesting a means to solve the housing problem in which the display of affordable materials and construction took on a more complex meaning.

After the crash of 1929, it became apparent that the individual house, even if (questionably) ideal, was economically unattainable for most Americans. Architects began to develop prototypes for prefabrication, with the intent of lowering costs—notably Grosvenor Attebury in 1907, Thomas Edison in 1908, R. Buckminster Fuller in the 1920s, Keck and Keck in the 1930s, and Konrad Wachsmann and Walter Gropius in the 1940s. These were not very successful economic ventures because so much financing was necessary to produce the assembly process for such little production.

Buckminster Fuller, however, challenged traditional forms and materials. He rationalized both structural and mechanical systems, minimizing work on the site— indeed, minimizing the relationship of the dwelling to the site altogether. After some early experiments with low-cost emergency housing, Fuller began developing his Dymaxion House in the 1920s (see fig. 2.25). The house was "named" by the Marshall Field's department store in Chicago to gain attention for a campaign to sell modern furniture. Fuller viewed himself as a visionary whose aim was to revolutionize the archaic existing system of construction, and he often seemed more inventor than architect. Although Fuller had earlier proposed stacking the Dymaxion unit into a tower (shipped to the site by dirigible), Mumford criticized the Dymaxion for still requiring substantial amounts of private property and not having anything to do with urban community.

The Aluminaire House, on the other hand, combined this spirit for innovation with the European progressive tradition. As such, a most distinguished hybrid was produced that was unparalleled in Europe or America. Fuller's work, while aimed at mass production, did not use standardized, available parts. The European mass-produced units looked as much like the site-constructed modern buildings as the American version looked traditional. The Aluminaire House, however, established a new image that combined the Fulleresque inventor-futurism with the European polemics.

Figure 2.25 "Dymaxian House" project, 1929, R. Buckminster Fuller.

THE ALUMINAIRE HOUSE AND LE CORBUSIER

There are several relationships that the Aluminaire House has to specific modern European housing projects. The predominant influence, however, is that of the work of Le Corbusier, with whom Albert Frey worked. The *Maison Dom-ino* diagram of 1915 demonstrated the idea of the free plan in the design of modern buildings with modern construction by using a concrete column grid and a one-way concrete slab (see fig. 2.5). This concept was used in the Aluminaire House in its aluminum framing elements (see fig. 1.41). The development of the "dom-ino" concept (units placed together like dominos) into the Maison Standardisee in 1923 (see fig. 2.27) is seen in Le Corbusier's 1924–26 housing at Pessac, France. This and the 1929 project for the back-to-back, steel-frame, prefabricated Loucheur houses that Frey worked on in Le Corbusier's office (see figs. 1.47 and 1.48) are critical precedents for the 1931 *Architectural Record* article by Kocher and Frey and the Aluminaire House (see fig. 2.3).

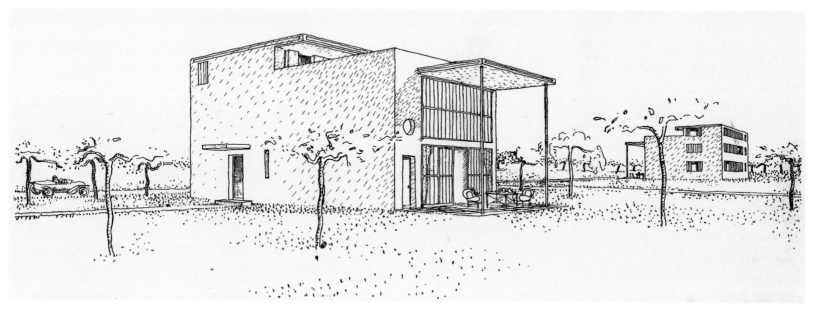

ABOVE AND OPPOSITE: Figure 2.26 Le Corbusier, Maison Citrohan project, 1920 and 1922.

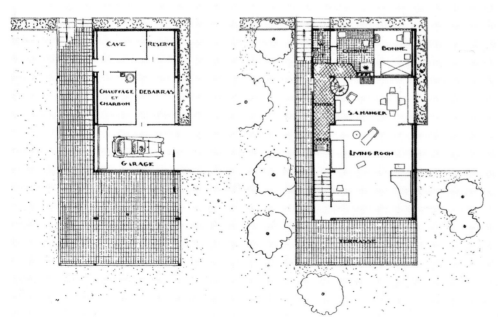

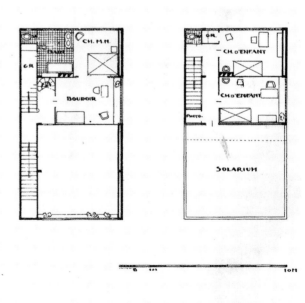

An important precedent to the Aluminaire House can be found in Le Corbusier's experimentation with repeatable units in his 1920 and 1922 Citrohan houses (see fig. 2.26), and also the Weissenhof unit, which consists of a column and slab structure with an open ground floor and a curved entry pavilion containing a stairway and exposed heating plant (see fig. 2.28). The second floor is the main living space and has a double-height living room facing a glass window wall, while the dining area is under a mezzanine containing a sitting room and bedroom. The entry stairway arrives at the intersection of the kitchen and dining room and continues, over itself, to the mezzanine. There is a roof terrace at the top level. All of these features are common to the Aluminaire House.

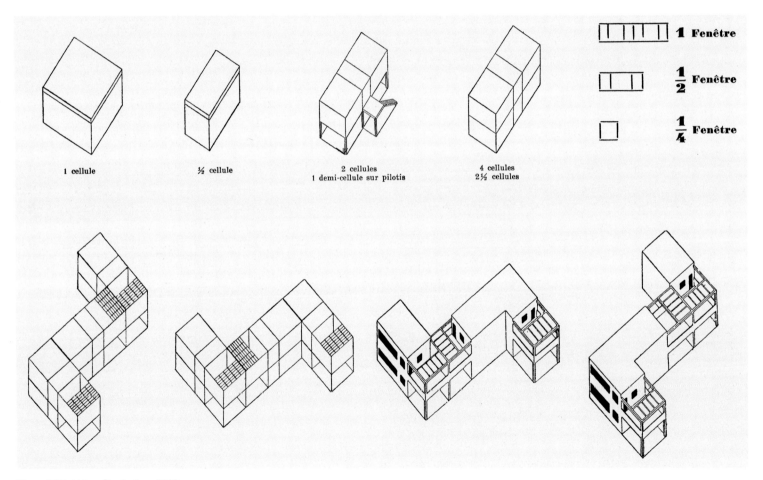

1 cellule   ½ cellule   2 cellules   4 cellules
                              1 demi-cellule sur pilotis   2½ cellules

1 Fenêtre

$\frac{1}{2}$ **Fenêtre**

$\frac{1}{4}$ **Fenêtre**

Figure 2.27 Maison Standardisee, 1923.

The nearly square plan of Le Corbusier's 1927 Maison Cooke, like that of the Aluminaire House, is a one-way cantilever with a central row of columns and a quadranted plan (see fig. 2.30). The cubic mass is raised off the ground on columns with the recessed, curved entry pavilion, and a roof terrace is cut out of the top next to a study. Although this is a design for a private house, its elements and structure relate to the strategies that Le Corbusier developed for housing solutions like the Citrohan and Weissenhof units. The Villa Stein (1927) at Garches is also a remarkable rendition of these housing projects, designed as a party wall building and transformed into a freestanding, upper-middle-class house (see fig. 2.31).These two canonical buildings of Le Corbusier have a relationship to the Aluminaire House in that they reflect Le Corbusier's housing strategies and organization and thus provide built examples as precedent for Frey.

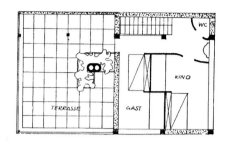

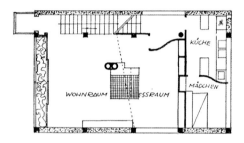

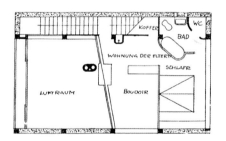

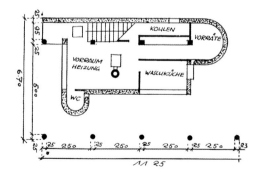

ABOVE AND RIGHT: Figure 2.28 Weisenhof Seidlung, Stuttgart, Germany, 1927, single house, view and plans.

Equally important to the Aluminaire is Le Corbusier's Esprit Nouveau pavilion for the 1925 Exposition Internationale des arts Decoratifs et Industiales in Paris (see fig. 2.29). The pavilion was a mock-up of his 1922 project for the Immeubles-Villas residential perimeter blocks. This, in turn, was transformed into larger courtyard superblock units and *redent*, bent slab building forms in the Ville Contemporaine ideal city plan (which was presented in a diorama pavilion attached to the Esprit Nouveau unit.) In the Esprit Nouveau, the nearly square plan is organized into quadrants. One side of the square was a Citrohan-type organization with double-height living room and window wall. The adjacent terrace quadrant brings the ground up in the air for high-rise living and is nearly identical to the terrace of Garches, including the opening to let light and air through the stacking of multiple units. The Immeubles-Villas is not entered through the front façade, but through the corridor connecting the units. In the exhibition unit, Le Corbusier transformed the exterior entry shared wall into a painted graphic façade. Entry circulation is thus through layered walls into the spaces of the unit that run within the layers. The Aluminaire House works with this same kind of rotation. In the Aluminaire House, entry through the front façade leads to a sequence of layered walls, arriving at the main living area of double-height space and window wall, in the back layer, which is perpendicular to this movement (see fig. 1.42, diagram 4).

ABOVE AND OPPOSITE: Figure 2.29 *Pavillon de l'Esprit Nouveau, Paris, 1925, exterior and interior view and plans.*

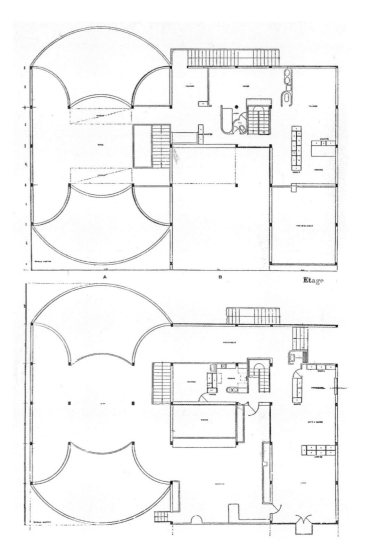

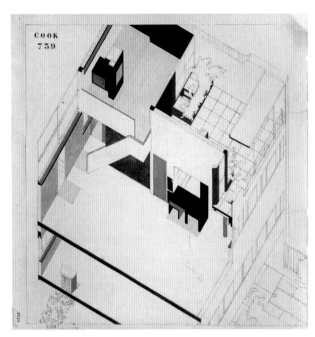

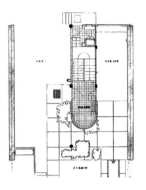

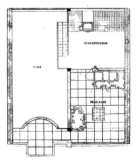

ABOVE AND RIGHT: Figure 2.30 Maison Cook, Paris, 1926.

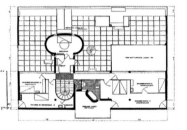

ABOVE AND RIGHT: Figure 2.31 Villa Stein at Garches.

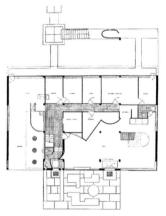

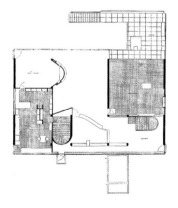

Photographs were taken by Albert Frey during the reconstruction (see figs. 3.2–3.10). He was on the site as an observer rather than by invitation to assist with the reconstruction. Construction photographs indicate summer foliage, while the photographs that were taken when the house was completed, which became the public images of the house, appear to have been taken in the late fall.

The December 6, 1931, *New York American* article was prophetic for the evolving significance of the house. Although the designers' names are mentioned, the article implies that the house was mainly Harrison's "experiment." Alongside images of Le Corbusier's housing at Pessac and Stuttgart, it discusses Harrison's entrepreneurial interest in mass producing low-cost suburban houses. He is quoted as saying, "mass production, mass buying and marketing holds the key to the future of the building industries"[10] (see fig. 3.1).

Figure 3.3 The Wallace Harrison reconstruction in 1931–1932, Huntington, Long Island, aluminum panels.

Figure 3.4 The Wallace Harrison reconstruction in 1931–1932, Huntington, Long Island, aluminum panels.

By 1931, however, like numerous other American architects, he began to develop an interest in modern architecture. When asked why Harrison bought the house, Albert Frey responded that he thought "he [Harrison] was interested in modern architecture, but he didn't know how to do it."[4] Harrison was known as a designer of office buildings. Other than his own house in Huntington, Long Island, he did not design in the modern style until the late 1930s.

So Harrison paid one thousand dollars and took the Aluminaire House in parts to Long Island. After the birth of their daughter, his wife apparently "pleaded for more space."[5] The *Brooklyn Daily Eagle* reported on June 1, 1931, that "it will be erected within the next week or ten days." It also stated, however, that Harrison had plans to add "a few additional rooms such as a guest room and a nursery," the preparation of which was "holding up the building work"[6] (see fig. 3.11). Other delays occurred as well. Harrison's biography notes that the aluminum panels were difficult to attach because the builders could not locate the wooden plugs to screw into.[7] Joseph Rosa's Frey monograph also notes that the parts were numbered according to a key plan but the numbers washed off in the rain.[8] Whatever the reasons, the house took several months to complete at a cost of $26,000 (including complex land preparation and the creation of a long driveway). A steam radiator system shop drawing for the house, dated October 1931, suggests that there may not have been heat that winter, and the Harrisons may not have planned to use the house in the winter in any case. A December 6 headline article in the Sunday Real Estate and Financial section of the *New York American* stated that it would not be occupied until the following spring.[9]

Figure 3.2 The Wallace Harrison reconstruction in 1931–1932, Huntington, Long Island, aluminum frame.

THE KOCHER-FRYE HOUSE AT SYOSSET, LONG ISLAND, DISCARDS
TRADITIONS OF CONSTRUCTION AND LOOKS IN AN EFFORT TO
PROVIDE THE MODERN LOW-COST HOME

Figure 3.1 Wallace Harrison publishes the Aluminaire as a suburban house of his own design.

THE WEEKEND HOUSE

Among the 135,000 visitors to the Aluminaire House in April 1931 was Wallace Harrison, an emerging American architect who lived from 1895 to 1981. His better-known works include an involvement with the Rockefeller Center plan, the United Nations Headquarters, the plan for Lincoln Center with its Metropolitan Opera, and the Albany State Government Mall.

Wallace K. Harrison was born in Worchester, Massachusetts, in 1895. He was ten years younger than Kocher and eight years older than Frey. He worked for an architectural firm in Worchester, studied structural engineering, and in 1916 was in New York working for McKim Mead and White and studying at the Harvey Wiley Corbett atelier. He attended the Ecole de Beaux-Arts briefly in 1921. In 1922 he worked for Bertram Grosvenor Goodhue and in 1927 started the firm Helmle, Corbett and Harrison. In 1929 this firm and others started the Rockefeller Center design that began construction in 1931, the year of the exhibition of the Aluminaire House.[1]

Harrison was possibly drawn to what he saw in the Grand Central Palace for two reasons. One was an interest in a small weekend house, as he and his wife had grown fond of weekend visits to Long Island. In 1931 he bought property in Huntington-Syosset, and they wanted to build something quickly before the birth of their daughter that May. With the notion that the Aluminaire House could be taken down, easily moved, and erected in what he, Kocher, and Frey thought would be eighteen days (six to seven days after getting the parts "ready for assembly"), Harrison must have seen the house as a good solution to his problem.[2]

The second possible reason for Harrison's interest in this particular house was his growing curiosity about modern architecture. In 1926 Harrison was more interested in art deco architecture when he visited the Metropolitan Museum of Art installation of the 1925 Paris Exposition des Arts Decoratifs et Industriels Modernes than in Le Corbusier's Esprit Nouveau Pavilion, which he felt "looked as if it had left history behind, it made a complete cut with the past for Corb's own ideas."[3]

3

THE HARRISON HOUSE—1932

According to the article, Harrison was proud of the radical style of the house and felt "that just as fashions are created in dress and people made to like it, so they may be created in architecture."[11] Harrison's designs for his own house, which was started after 1932 as an addition to the Aluminaire House, had stucco walls, large steel and glass windows, and a flat roof (see figs. 3.12–3.14), with a rather naïve interest in merging circles into rectangular forms. Although Harrison did not build a modern building himself until the late 1930s, the *New York American* article suggests that Harrison had taken possession of the idea of the house. Its past was about to be erased in its forthcoming publicity.

LEFT: Figure 3.5 The Wallace Harrison reconstruction in 1931–1932, Huntington, Long Island, the roof terrace.

RIGHT: Figure 3.6 The Wallace Harrison reconstruction in 1931–1932, Huntington, Long Island, the entry terrace.

MODERN ARCHITECTURE—INTERNATIONAL EXHIBITION AT THE MUSEUM OF MODERN ART

ALUMINAIRE HOUSE, first built at Architectural League Show, New York, later taken down and re-erected as a country home at Syosset, Long Island. Entirely dry construction: light steel and aluminium frame; units designed for standardisation.

Just about the time in 1931 when Harrison was completing the construction of the Aluminaire House on Long Island, Philip Johnson modified his original ideas for the 1932 Museum of Modern Art's Modern Architecture–International Exhibition, to include a group of ancillary examples that would show the extent of the spread of the so-called International Style. Philip Johnson, Henry-Russell Hitchcock Jr., and Alfred Barr were anxious to include American work, and along with the inclusions of Frank Lloyd Wright, Howe and Lescaze, the Bowman brothers, and Richard Neutra (in place of the original choice of Norma Bel Geddes), six selections from the United States comprised this section of the exhibition.

How the Aluminaire House was selected for inclusion is not clear. The house must have been prominent among so few examples, which included a gas station. Philip Johnson had seen the Aluminaire House in the exhibition that he had demonstrated against in April, and, ironically, that may have led to its selection. Johnson probably knew Harrison through their mutual Rockefeller connections. The Rockefeller family headed the Board of Trustees of the Museum, and Harrison was related to the family and worked for them throughout his career.[12]

Figure 3.7 The Aluminaire House in 1932, Huntington, Long Island, front façade, as pictured in *The Modern House* by F. R. S. Yorke in 1934.

OPPOSITE

LEFT: Figure 3.8 The Harrison House in 1932, Huntington, Long Island, front and primary side façade.

CENTER: Figure 3.9 The Harrison House in 1932, Huntington, Long Island, front and side façade.

RIGHT: Figure 3.10 The Harrison House in 1932, Huntington, Long Island, primary side and back façade.

Although the drawings and possibly the photograph by Albert Frey were used in the exhibition and publications, there was nothing in the Kocher archive to suggest that Kocher or Frey were consulted. The house was labeled the "Harrison House, Syosset, Long Island, 1931," and no mention is made of the Aluminaire House or the Architectural League and Allied Arts and Industries exhibition. The house must have been a thorn in Johnson's side as it did not fit into the argument of his demonstration against the League the previous spring. However, he co-opted its success by selecting it for the MoMA exhibition after it was rebuilt in October 1931. By choosing to call it the Harrison House, the Museum of Modern Art exhibition erased its previous history. Here, at the moment of the building's most significant exposure, the name Aluminaire House was dropped. Gone also was any reference to mass production or low-cost housing. In their place emerged an image of a weekend house in a wooded, pre-suburban, eleven-acre setting (see figs. 3.7–3.10).

Lewis Mumford posed the issues of housing in his contribution to the MoMA catalog's housing section of the 1932 exhibition (not originally planned) that was organized by Mumford, Catherine Bauer, Henry Wright, and Clarence Stein. This could have included "the House of the Future." The Harrison House, instead, is presented as an example of the International Style. Being included in the "style" section, it was not accompanied by any of the polemical background on housing that was critical to the Aluminaire's inception. This disconnection had begun in the League show in which the double agenda of exhibiting materials in an interesting way may have hidden or compromised the more controversial issue of the prototype for affordable housing. Unfortunately, Kocher and Frey's concept of the House within the context of housing was presented simultaneously, but remotely, in their *Architectural Record* article of April 1931. Le Corbusier had his arguments about housing and the city as dioramas in the pavilion attached to the Esprit Nouveau exhibition house in Paris in 1925. Perhaps Kocher and Frey had less conviction, leaving the relationship more implicit than explicit as had Le Corbusier, but Johnson certainly played a significant role in its disappearance. The Harrison House was presented as precisely what Mumford rejected in his debates of 1931, a house for "the romantic individual nourished in the illusion of isolation"—the opposite of the promise of the Aluminaire House as a unit from which communities could be formed.

TOP: **Figure 3.11** Addition to the Aluminaire House by Wallace Harrison in 1932.

BOTTOM: **Figure 3.12** Wallace Harrison at work in the yard, *Life* magazine, April 1935.

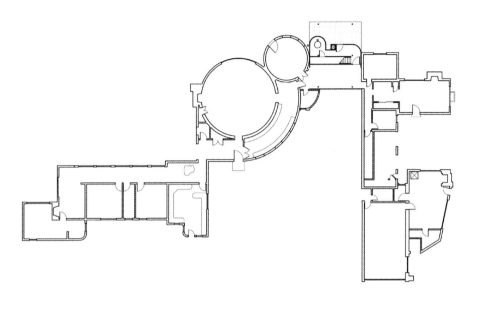

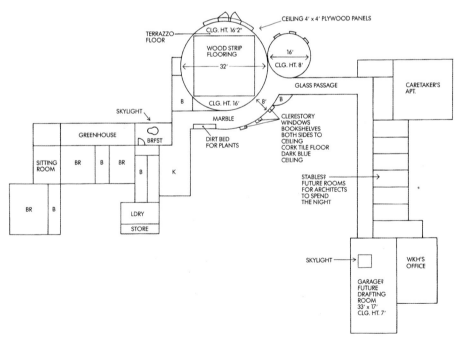

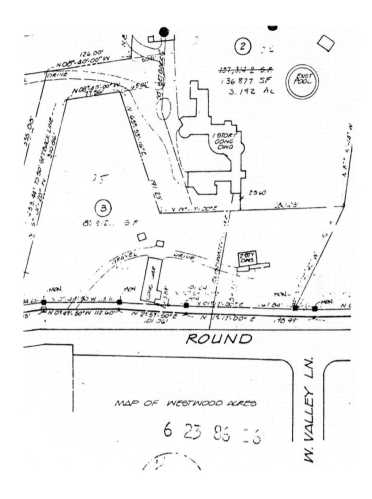

ABOVE LEFT: **Figure 3.13** Plan of the Harrison House with the Aluminaire House as interpreted from the renovation plans by Schappacher-White, 2006.

LEFT: **Figure 3.14** Diagram in *Wallace Harrison Architect.*

ABOVE RIGHT: **Figure 3.15** Survey site plan of the Harrison estate indicating the location of the relocated Aluminaire House.

THE INTERNATIONAL STYLE PUBLICATION

In 1932, Henry-Russell Hitchcock Jr. and Philip Johnson, under the aegis of the Museum of Modern Art, published *The International Style: Architecture Since 1922*. It began in 1930 as a proposal to make a more accessible version of Hitchcock's *Modern Architecture: Romanticism and Reintegration* of 1929. The work on this publication was in conjunction with the MoMA exhibition of that year, which the authors organized with Alfred Barr. The Hitchcock-Johnson book actually hid or subverted the intentions of modernism by analyzing and establishing critical criteria with the kinds of aesthetic terms that were common to the beaux arts, while castigating the functionalists. "While the functionalists continue to deny the aesthetic element in architecture as important, more and more buildings are produced in which these principles are wisely and effectively followed without sacrifice of functional virtues."[13]

The book proposed three principles, or issues, of analysis, criticism, and design itself. These are volume, regularity, and avoidance or absence of applied decoration or ornament. Each is discussed in terms of visual effect and argued as an aesthetic issue. In their flagrant and continuous criticism of the "fanatical functionalist," Hitchcock and Johnson also avoided discussing the movement in terms of any connection to social issues.

Interested in the early modern European canonical buildings, as well as the emerging, more populist, second phase of the modern movement, Hitchcock and Johnson presented a subtle and insidious revision that transformed the polemics of the modern movement from functionalism and constructivism—developed through a strong political conviction and ideological position of concern for the working class—into an argument founded on aesthetics.

They attempted to disconnect architectural form-making from other forces in society, as well as from the other architectonic issues that were essential for the making of modern architecture in its first phase. Their book presented, in fact, a return to ideas that were in place before the modern movement began. "The arguments of the functionalists are not based on the actual situation in the contemporary world outside of Russia. Whether they ought to or not, many clients can still afford architecture in addition to building."[14]

The interest in egalitarianism, which brought attention to concerns for the fundamental dwelling, was replaced by an interest in advanced capitalism and consumption. "An architecture, aristocratic rather than puritanical, may arise sometimes on an Acropolis in all of the luxury of Pentelic marble and yet will grace with distinction the factory and the *Siedlung*."[15]

Thanks to Hitchcock and Johnson, America was thus introduced to the modern movement with the designation "International Style," with the definition and criteria established by their own publication. It is therefore no coincidence that at the same time that modern architecture was proclaimed the International Style, the Aluminaire House—or the "House of the Future"—became the Harrison weekend house in Syosset, Long Island. It was entirely consistent with the demise of the controversy over the modern movement (see fig. 3.16).

The concerns of modernism, embodied in the Aluminaire House, to address both urbanism and housing, with both a social and a visual statement, were thus masked if not buried. Likewise, a style that grew out of, and was formed by metaphorical, if not literal relationships to functionalism, constructivism, radical politics, and art movements was

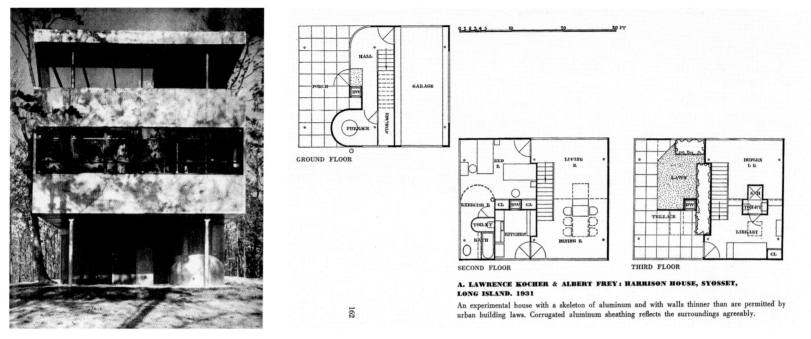

GROUND FLOOR

SECOND FLOOR

THIRD FLOOR

A. LAWRENCE KOCHER & ALBERT FREY: HARRISON HOUSE, SYOSSET, LONG ISLAND. 1931

An experimental house with a skeleton of aluminum and with walls thinner than are permitted by urban building laws. Corrugated aluminum sheathing reflects the surroundings agreeably.

162

Figure 3.16 Frontal view and plans from *The International Style: Architecture Since 1922*, Henry Russell Hitchcock Jr. and Philip Johnson, 1932. There were only six American projects and only two houses in the book.

subverted and revised into aesthetics. The avoidance of modernism's critical criteria and its replacement with aesthetic issues set it up for easy criticism and was in part responsible for the loss of interest in the Aluminaire. This, combined with the collapse of the *zeitgeist* that sought a new modern society, culture, and politics, ushered in an acceptance of the status quo and a review of the role of the architect as simply solving and not questioning or expanding "the program" in social terms. From 1932 until our work began, the Aluminaire House has remained known as a curious bourgeois weekend house and, as such, exemplifies the course of modern architectural theory. Once isolated from its theoretical, philosophical, and political foundations in the 1930s, the International Style became an easy target to the constant barrage of criticism, occurring since the 1960s, proclaiming its demise and the need for more up-to-date styles.

In essence, the Aluminaire House can be considered as having had a history of being in the wrong place at the right time. Shown in the Architectural League/Allied Arts and Industry Exhibition, it probably belonged in the Rejected Architects Exhibition. Although it was included in the pivotal 1932 Museum of Modern Art exhibition, it was positioned as an example of International Style architecture in America, whereas it might have been more appropriately placed in the "housing" section. In this way, although possibly in a less prestigious position in the exhibition, it would have remained a part of the critical debate surrounding housing and urban planning that escaped the Hitchcock/ Johnson whitewash. It could have truly fulfilled Catherine Bauer's fantasy of modern architecture making modern towns.

4

THE HOUSE 1932–2014

LOST: 1932–1986

A single photograph in the Lawrence Kocher archive (see fig. 3.11), and another from an article on Wallace Harrison in an April 1935 issue of *Life* magazine (see fig. 3.12), show the addition to the Aluminaire House, which must have begun during the spring of 1932[1] (see fig. 3.12). A new thirty-two-foot diameter living room and adjacent circular dining room, rather than the reported nursery and guest room, were constructed. The addition was off to the two sides of the Aluminaire House, in the location of the two side garage doors (see fig. 3.11).[2] The *Life* article attests to Harrison's significance in American culture and society by displaying his house and way of life.

Around 1940, when a new wing of bedrooms was added to the living/dining area, the Aluminaire House was moved down the steep hill which ran from the original house site to the main road (see fig. 3.15). How it was moved seems to have gone unrecorded and it is very difficult to imagine the move. When the house was taken down later in 1987, evidence indicated that it had not been dismantled again.[3]

Thus, it seemed that Harrison lost interest in the house, or in maintaining its integrity. It would have had to be pushed or dragged to its new location, about one hundred fifty feet away on the steep slope. Rather than adjust the land, the house itself was radically altered by removing the entire ground floor. The six columns were cut, and the remaining house was placed on a cement block basement and garage, which was mostly below grade.

Except for the 1934 publication *The Modern House*, by F. R. S. Yorke in England[4] (with reprintings in 1935 and 1937), which included a detailed report of the house, there is nothing recorded about the Aluminaire House from 1932 to the late 1960s. It appears in no other books discussing modern architecture or in the histories of the modern movement.

In Reynor Banham's 1969 book, *The Architecture of the Well-Tempered Environment*, the Aluminaire House is mentioned and although there is a suggestion of familiarity with the house, it is doubtful that he ever saw it.

It is not known when the various changes to the house occurred after the move down the hill in the 1940s. A drawing exists with some of these changes, but it is undated, so it does not help reconstruct the chronology of events. Harrison apparently rented the house to friends or employees. In 1974, art dealers Harold and Hester Diamond bought the estate and lived in the Harrison house while continuing to rent out the Aluminaire.[5] They sold the property to Dr. Joel Karen, a plastic surgeon, in 1984. Because of his interest in developing the site through subdivision, Karen planned to demolish the Aluminaire House, and he received a demolition permit from the town of Huntington for that purpose on October 10, 1986.

FOUND: DECONSTRUCTION AND RECONSTRUCTION, 1987–1997

The Huntington Historical Society, directed by Rufus Langhorn, was the first to take note of the intention to demolish the house and wanted to prevent it, as the Aluminaire House, along with the whole Harrison estate, had been placed on the National Register of Historic Places in 1985.[6] The Society alerted the Long Island Chapter of the American Institute of Architects (AIA). Hugh Gershon, then president of the chapter, contacted Paul Goldberger, architecture editor for the *New York Times*. On March 8, 1987, Goldberger wrote a small article on the Aluminaire House, which included an image, in the Sunday Arts and Leisure section of the *New York Times*. Joseph Rosa, a recent architecture graduate, was nearing completion of a book on Albert Frey's work and became very involved in the issue.[7] The Long Island AIA also contacted people that it thought might be able to save the house from imminent demolition. One such contact was on February 20, 1987, to Julio M. San Jose, dean of the School of Architecture at New York Institute of Technology (NYIT). Since I (Jon Michael Schwarting) had an interest in the house, I became chairperson of architecture at the Islip campus of that school in the summer of 1987. (Note: From this point, the authors become part of the history of the house.) I knew of the house from an interest in its construction while working on metal panel research as an associate in the architectural office of Richard Meier in the early 1970s. I visited the house in 1975 with students as associate professor in the Graduate School of Architecture, Planning and Preservation, at Columbia University. In 1986, the house was in nearly the same condition, except for its abandoned state, as it was in the 1970s (see figs. 4.1–4.10)

Figure 4.1 Living room side with replaced panels and door cut into living room window wall.

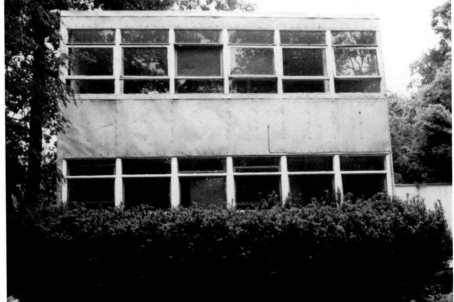

OPPOSITE

LEFT: Figure 4.2 Living room side with garage below and added porch and new entry door into living room.

UPPER RIGHT: Figure 4.3 Front with enclosed upper terrace, missing ground floor, and side with kitchen entry.

LOWER RIGHT: Figure 4.4 Front with added upper terrace and lower garage in basement.

TOP: Figure 4.5 View from dining to living room with filled-in double-height space, encased chrome column for plumbing, and supports for glass case and roll-out dining table.

BOTTOM: Figure 4.6 Former terrace enclosed with wood frame windows.

TOP: **Figure 4.7** View to upper bedroom over living room.

BOTTOM: **Figure 4.8** Living room with double-height space enclosed. The chrome columns have been encased.

OPPOSITE

TOP: **Figure 4.9** View into the upper bathroom.

BOTTOM: **Figure 4.10** View into main bathroom with toilet enclosure.

Figure 4.11 Removing the windows in the front façade.

Figure 4.12 Removing the windows and panels of the front of the house.

An application was made by NYIT to the New York State Department of Parks, Recreation, and Historic Preservation for a preservation grant, available through the 1986 New York State Environmental Quality Bond Act. On May 26, 1987, with the understanding that the owner would give the house to NYIT (with the provision that it be moved quickly), the Huntington Historical Society agreed to its removal from the town of Huntington. The NYIT Board of Trustees and its president, Dr. Matthew Schure, accepted the responsibility to remove and reconstruct the house, and the grant application was submitted in June 1987. On August 28, 1987, the application was awarded the first grant for preservation of a modern building by New York State. As modern architecture was just being recognized as historically significant, it was unusual that this fifty-year-old example would receive such recognition. Michael Lynch, director of the New York State Department of Parks, Recreation, and Historic Preservation, was very interested in the project and instrumental in the awarding of the grant.[8]

The proposal itself was both complex and unorthodox. It specified saving the house through an educational and teaching structure within the context of the architecture school. Students would, among other things, do the work of removal and saving the house as one aspect of a larger concept of executing its rebuilding. The courses of instruction were also dedicated to teaching issues of history, preservation, design, and construction. Thus, the specific act of saving the house was the first phase of a larger project agenda for a greater awareness of the issues of affordable housing, how these issues were approached in the modern movement, and, hopefully, how the ongoing problem of housing could be approached in the present and future. Upon completion of the restoration, the house was to be open to the public and managed by the school as a museum.

As director of the project and chairperson of the school, I had the responsibility of structuring the project, executing the grant, and teaching the requisite courses. Frances Campani, an architect on Long Island and adjunct professor at Columbia University, came to NYIT to teach and become associate director of the project, responsible for coordinating the documentation and legal approvals. Paul Field, a NYIT alumnus with a construction company in Port Jefferson, Long Island, took an adjunct faculty position to assist in teaching the part of the course that involved the dismantling, moving, and reconstruction of the house.

A strategic plan, modeled on the methods used in archeology, was developed for the deconstruction work, and the house was photographically documented in the fall and winter of 1987. The house was documented, dismantled, and moved in three semesters between January 1988 and May 1989 (see figs. 4.11–4.24). Because of the obligation to remove the house as quickly as possible, Paul Field Construction Company worked in the summer of 1988 to remove all of the aluminum and cement panels, windows, roofing, and a chimney.

The archaeological system of mapping a grid on the site as an abstract matrix to reference things was altered to divide the house into its constituent parts. Students were responsible for their segments and each layer of construction fabric was carefully documented in notes, drawings, and photographs before its removal, revealing the subsequent layer. The first layer was the wall and ceiling fabric (canvas rather than Fabrikoid) and linoleum flooring on the inside, and the metal and cement panels as well as the windows on the outside. Next was the "building paper" on the outside, followed by the insulation panels on both outside and inside. This then revealed the steel girt system and wood nailers as well as the girders and beams. The floor sound insulation and steel decking, as well as the roofing and windows, had to be removed before this structural system could be dismantled. Drafted drawings were made from sketches, which then were translated into digital construction drawings. Thus the system of recording and documentation of the deconstruction of the existing became the basis for the reconstruction.

Figure 4.13 Removing the windows and panels of the front of the house.

UPPER LEFT: Figure 4.14 View of the girts, nailers, and frame at the front and side of the house.

LOWER LEFT: Figure 4.15 View from the living room with the stair up to the library.

RIGHT: Figure 4.16 View of the upper part of the living room with the upper bathroom off the library.

Figure 4.17 View of the double-height space of the living room.

The changes Harrison had made to the house obscured much of the character and original design of the house. There was nothing left of the ground floor. It had been replaced by the cement block basement that, because of the slope of the terrain, was completely underground on the south, east, and north sides—exposed only on the west side (see fig. 4.1). A garage was located in this exposed area of the basement, and it was accessible through hinged wood doors approximately where one of the original garage doors had been located. A porch had been welded to the house above the garage, with a door installed through the lower right window of the living room window wall, opposite the stairway (see fig. 4.2). A second door, with a roof shed, had been added in place of one of the kitchen windows next to the dining room (see fig. 4.3). A small, curved wall had been added to the kitchen to accommodate this entry. The kitchen contained none of its original equipment or cabinetry, and there was no evidence of the dumbwaiter until one of the doors was found later in the dismantling. In the dining room, the chrome pipes to the upper bathroom were hidden in square wood boxing. The glass cabinet with its dining table was missing. Windows on the second floor, as well as the new ones on the third (where there were none originally) had been boxed out to accept wood-frame screens. The double-height living room was divided by a wood-framed floor to form a bedroom at the third level (see figs. 4.5–4.8). The ceiling of the revised living room and the dining room had glued-on acoustical tiles. In the bathroom, only the toilet cabinet remained of the original fixtures. The new fixtures dated from the 1950s, and the walls on two sides of the bathtub were tiled. The original medicine cabinet, seen in the Frey sketches, and the mirror he designed were not there. The exercise screen (except for a track later found in the floor), the closets—presumably like the ones Kocher and Frey wrote about in *Architectural Record*—and the suspended beds were also missing.

The new third-floor bedroom over the living room was entered at the location of the original balcony parapet and cabinetry adjacent to the stairs, while the cabinetry on the other side of the upper bathroom had been converted into a closet (see fig. 4.7). The original closet in the back corner of the library had been enlarged over earlier plans. The bathroom was entirely tiled and had new fixtures in it, leaving no evidence of what it had once been like. The wire glass skylights had been replaced by the newer plastic bubble type. The upper terrace had been enclosed and made into another bedroom. The front opening above the parapet was enclosed with wood frame windows and the once-open ends (sides) of the terrace were enclosed with solid walls (see fig. 4.6). Thus the signature diagonal wall had disappeared from view. (Its framing was found within the wall later.) A continuous row of closets had been installed along the central column zone where originally a planter on the open terrace had been planned. A metal chimney, originally designed to be outside the building, extended from the basement through the second-floor bedroom closets next to the kitchen, and finally through these new upper closets. In order to accommodate the new bedroom, the inner diagonal-shaped wall on the terrace with the fold-down table and the dumbwaiter had been removed. Newly added walls and floors were framed in wood. Gypsum board, which was not available in 1931 (and probably would not have been used because Frey avoided labor-intensive detailing), was used for all the new construction. New electrical cable was found in the walls, cut into the insulation board, and had made its way to new outlets and switches. The original neon and ultraviolet lighting above the living room window was also gone, and there was no evidence that it had ever been reinstalled after the exhibition.

All the DuPont Fabrikoid wall fabric had been replaced by canvas at reconstruction. Although every wall and ceiling was painted white, there was some evidence that the rooms had been various colors at some time. The outside surfaces of the third-floor shower, which once faced out over the living room but were now part of the new upper bedroom, were pink and blue, painted in a nonsymmetrical pattern, and the library ceiling had been a dark blue before being painted the white that was found in 1987. The linoleum, which according to Albert Frey had been all gray in the exhibition, was black throughout, a change which probably was made in 1931 when the house was rebuilt. A 1960s or 1970s oil-fired steam boiler had been installed in the basement with an adjacent hot-water heater. Contemporary fin-tube heating was found in the living room in custom-made, oversized, perforated aluminum covers that once probably shielded radiators. Cast-iron radiators were found with similar covers in the dining room and bedroom and exposed in the upper floor as well as the ceiling of the garage. The radiators in the newer terrace bedroom were enclosed in built-in wood and perforated metal cabinetry along the original outer parapet (see figs. 4.5 and 4.6). The heating system followed a 1931 shop drawing that was found in the house. This was designed for Harrison, as there had been no heating system specified for the exhibition house. There was an air-conditioning system on the roof feeding the upper-floor rooms.[9]

Figure 4.22 Columns and frame detail of connections.

As the deconstruction progressed, the parts were periodically loaded onto an NYIT truck and moved eighteen miles to the NYIT Central Islip campus and stored. The Central Islip campus was relatively new, having opened in 1984 with the purchase of a closed-down New York State psychiatric hospital. The architecture program served as a satellite to programs at the two other campuses and was located in a building that had housed tuberculosis patients, known as the Sunburst Building. Consisting of twelve wings on two quarter-circle hallways flanking a central pavilion, the architecture program occupied two wings and the Aluminaire House was stored in another, undeveloped wing. This allowed enough space to systematically organize all the building elements. Before reconstruction began in the spring semester of 1990, students worked on preparing the architectural elements. This included sandblasting the steel parts of the structural frame, girts, and windows.

During the deconstruction, several materials could not be saved. This helped the students understand what the situation was like in its previous deconstruction in the Grand Central Palace and its reconstruction on the Harrison property. Although the exterior aluminum panels were substantially damaged due to Harrison's modifications of the house, they were carefully removed and stored. On the inside, the canvas wall covering glued to the insulation panels (which was not the original Fabrikoid) could not be saved. Similarly, neither the nonoriginal acoustical tile ceiling panels nor the ceiling insulation panels they were glued to were salvageable. The linoleum flooring could not be taken up intact and its acoustical underlayment had adhered to the steel floor decking. Significant rust had occurred to the decking, possibly caused by the underlayment, or possibly from being outside for a period of time during the Harrison reconstruction.

There was also a lot of missing material: aluminum panels from the Harrison modifications, exterior and interior doors, windows that had been replaced by doors at the kitchen and living room window wall, the curved glass at the entry, skylights, dumbwaiter, the entire kitchen, dining table, plumbing fixtures, entry terrace stone pavers, roof terrace asphalt pavers, and the Fabrikoid wall covering. None of the built-in fittings that Frey had designed, except for the aluminum toilet enclosure in the second-floor bathroom, were found.

On October 31, 1989, an application for regranting the project with the New York State Department of Parks, Recreation, and Historic Preservation funds was submitted, and the grant was awarded on February 20, 1990. The Alcoa Foundation of the Alcoa Aluminum Company of America in Pittsburg, Pennsylvania, also gave the project a grant on May 31, 1990.[10]

LEFT: Figure 4.23 Column and spaced girder.
RIGHT: Figure 4.24 Columns: the last things standing.

After the house was completely dismantled, moved, and stored, and while the materials were being prepped, the foundation was dug, and the perimeter and six footings were poured. The aluminum and steel frame, stairs, girt system, and new floor decking were prepared and erected, and the slab was poured in five semesters from September 1989 to December 1991 (see figs. 4.25–4.29). The work was suspended in December 1991 in order to complete and receive approval for a Historic Structures Report and draft nomination for the National Register, which was completed in October 1995.[11] Construction on the house resumed in April 1997.

ABOVE: Figure 4.25 Site staked out at Central Islip Campus of NYIT, 1990.

UPPER RIGHT: Figure 4.26 Foundations at a corner and column bases.

CENTER RIGHT: Figure 4.27 Foundations with the school of architecture behind.

LOWER RIGHT: Figure 4.28 Foundations at the entry and niche for the boiler.

Figure 4.29 The frame in fall 1993.

Figure 4.30 The structural frame and girts, 1993.

Figure 4.31 The frame with girts and nailers, 1996.

Figure 4.32 Building paper, 1997.

Figure 4.33 Installing the metal panels, 1998.

Figure 4.34 Enclosed, 2006.

Figure 4.35 Enclosed.

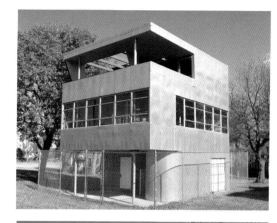

Figure 4.36 Enclosed, three views.

The courses were organized from 1988 to 1991 to accomplish both intellectual and physical work. Besides dismantling and reconstructing the house, students documented the house as they found it as well as how it was to be rebuilt, under the supervision of Professor Frances Campani. The students were assigned to do research on the materials that were originally utilized and the materials that would be used for substitutions where required. Besides issues related specifically to the construction of the house, the students studied and documented other houses and projects from the history of affordable housing and issues of mass production in the twentieth century with Professor Schwarting. This work was to become an archive of information that would be accessible in the rebuilt house once it opened as a museum.

UPPER ROW, LEFT TO RIGHT

Figure 4.37 Living room and stair to library and entry.

Figure 4.38 Living, dining, and kitchen with stair to library.

Figure 4.39 Living and dining room.

Figure 4.40 Living room looking up to library.

BOTTOM ROW, LEFT TO RIGHT

Figure 4.41 Bedroom and bathroom.

Figure 4.42 Library looking to double-height living room.

Figure 4.43 Library looking to double-height living room.

Figure 4.44 Upper terrace.

Figure 4.45 Sunset, 2000.

Annual events at NYIT were structured around the Aluminaire House to discuss its issues and importance. In 1993, its sixty-second birthday was celebrated with a lecture by Kenneth Frampton and remarks and observations about the house by Philip Johnson, Terrence Riley, Joseph Rosa, Tod Williams, Joan Ockman, and Steven Holl. It also celebrated the iconic moment of the completion of the structural frame. Subsequent events featured presentations by Christian Otto, coauthor of *The Wiessenhof Siedlung*; Guillame Julian de la Fuente, who worked in Le Corbusier's office from 1959 to 1965; and also Charles Gwathmey, Michael Graves, Tod Williams, Michael Sorkin.

During the deconstruction process, many questions and thoughts arose about the original exhibition house. The information in the press at the time of the exhibition was helpful but incomplete. There was little architectural press coverage or writing about the building after the exhibition and no discussions about construction or even descriptions of the physical exhibition house. Because of this, it was decided to write to Albert Frey about the restoration project and ask questions about its construction. Letters were exchanged and we realized that a recorded, in-person interview would be a much better way to have the necessary discussion. From May 26 to May 28, 1994, we (Jon Michael Schwarting and Frances Campani) visited with Albert Frey in his home in Palm Springs, California, to discuss the house as well as Frey's biography, work, and thoughts about architecture and life in general. Although ninety-two years of age, Frey had an amazing memory of the design and physical construction and character of the building. There was also the opportunity to visit Frey's work in Palm Springs, and it was possible to examine the transformation of his thinking over time, particularly in relation to the desert climate and physical character and mountain conditions. Certain continuities were noted, particularly in the employment of aluminum, even on the Palm Springs Town Hall, and invigorating conversations ensued over materials, colors, scale, and forms and, most important, invention. After our visit, we did additional research in the Kocher archives in Williamsburg, Virginia, in January 1995.

The documentation for the project has been exhibited in Barcelona, Spain, at the DOCOMOMO conference in 1994. It was included in an exhibition of the work of Albert Frey, curated by Joseph Rosa, and held in Lausanne and Zurich, Switzerland. The work was also exhibited periodically at NYIT.

In 1996 we made a proposal to the Architectural League of New York to create an exhibition about the house for its sixty-fifth anniversary. Since it was originally exhibited in conjunction with the 1931 League biennial exhibition, it seemed an appropriate venue. I (Michael) had been on the executive committee of the League in 1980–84. The exhibition, which took place in September 1997, consisted of a frieze of black-and-white photographs of the process of the work to document, deconstruct, store, and reconstruct the house. Black-and white-photographs of the 1931–32 Harrison reconstruction were included along with several framed drawings by Albert Frey, on loan from the Kocher archive in Williamsburg, Virginia. The exhibition also included large digital images of what the house once looked like and would look like again when rebuilt. Digital construction drawings by NYIT students for the ongoing reconstruction were exhibited.

THE SEARCH FOR ALUMINAIRE HOUSE SITES, 2005–2009

NYIT moved the School of Architecture and most other departments from its Central Islip campus in 2005. We investigated alternate locations for the Aluminaire House as well as alternate models for custodianship.

Discussions occurred with NYIT about moving the house to the Old Westbury campus, and that option was considered until about 2006. In 2004, the possibility of moving the house to the Houses at Sagaponack was discussed. This is a community of modern contemporary houses on Long Island still being developed. Richard Meier, who did the site plan for the project, liked the idea, and the organization applied to put it on a specific portion of the site. However, that proposal was turned down by the South Hampton Planning Department. Harry "Coco" Brown, the developer of the project, died in November 2005, and discussions with the new developers in 2007 were not fruitful.

In 2006, we discussed ideas for sites with developer Robert Rubin. Rubin is owner of the *Maison de Verre* in Paris, designed by Pierre Chareau, who also designed the Motherwell studio that was demolished in the Hamptons in the early 1980s. Rubin also donated a mass-producible metal Jean Prouvé house to the Centre Pompidou. A site in Ruben's development of a residential community in Riverhead, Long Island, an automobile raceway transformed into a golf community, was discussed but it was felt that this would not be a good public location or milieu for the house.

In 2008, there was discussion of relocating the house to a site in Southampton that was proposed for a museum of Long Island Modern Houses, with David Slater and Jake Gorst. Gorst is the grandson of Abraham Geller, whose Pearlroth house was being moved to this site. The project to create the museum did not materialize. Also in 2008 we made a public presentation to the Economic Development Corporation of Huntington, Long Island, to locate it in a proposed park in Huntington Station where there was an ongoing renewal project, but that also did not materialize. Sites were discussed with Barry Bergdoll, director of the Architecture and Design department of MoMA, Elise Quasebarth of Higgins and Quasebarth Preservation office, who produced the Historic Structures Report on the house, and others suggested giving it to a museum such as the Smithsonian Building Museum in Washington, DC, the Smithsonian Cooper Hewitt Design Museum in New York City, the Queens Museum in Flushing Meadows, New York, or the Vanderbilt Museum in Huntington, Long Island, but this was a complicated process, and the institutions did not have space for a project the size of the Aluminaire House at the time of those discussions.

In December 2008, we approached the developer of a site at 39th Avenue and 50th Street in Sunnyside, Queens, who had expressed interest in the Aluminaire, if approval could be granted from Landmarks Preservation Commission. Initial meetings with Landmarks staff in early 2009 generated a very positive response and they encouraged us to make a submission to the Commission. Drawings were required for zoning review by the Building Department, and were produced in our office, Campani and Schwarting Architects. It seemed that the project would be an excellent fit for both the Aluminaire House and the neighborhood.

THE ALUMINAIRE HOUSE FOUNDATION

While these site possibilities were considered, we formed a nonprofit corporation to take over the ownership and the responsibility for the house. The house was being vandalized due to insufficient security at the then-vacant Central Islip Campus. Once an appropriate new site was identified, it needed to be moved as quickly as possible. NYIT transferred the house to the Aluminaire House Foundation, Inc. on May 11, 2011. The officers of the Foundation were Jon Michael Schwarting, Kenneth Frampton, and Frances Campani.

THE SUNNYSIDE GARDENS INTERLUDE, 2010–2014

The Queens site was a vacant 100 by 100-foot lot facing a partial block of Sunnyside Gardens houses to the west and Phipps Garden Apartments to the north. The site was an abandoned playground for the residents of Phipps and had not been used for more than a decade when it was sold to a private developer. The developer proposed residential units for the site but was having difficulty gaining approval from the Landmarks Preservation Commission. The LPC staff expressed interest in having the Aluminaire House as part of the site plan, and the developer agreed to a joint venture of the project. The design situated the Aluminaire on the corner in a park-like setting with new apartment buildings creating an appropriate backdrop for the Aluminaire and compatible with the surrounding context. A walkway with park benches would surround the Aluminaire House and provide access to the residential units.

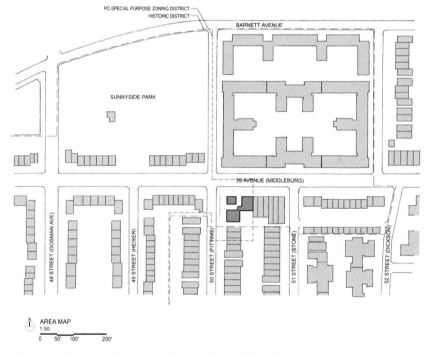

Figure 4.46 Sunnyside Gardens plan, Sunnyside Park and Phipps Houses. The Aluminaire site is at the corner of 39th Avenue and 50th Street.

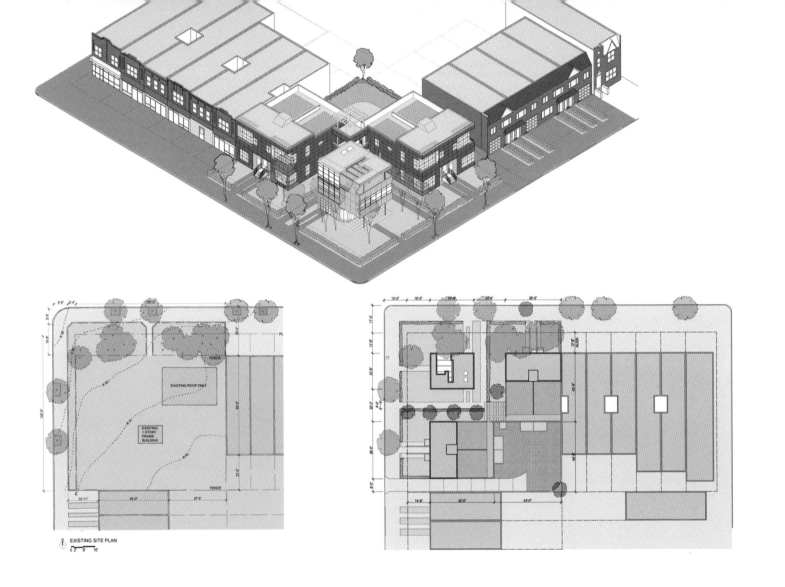

EXISTING SITE PLAN

Sunnyside Gardens was designed and built from 1924 to 1928 by Clarence S. Stein, Henry Wright, architect Frederick Lee Ackerman, and landscape architect Marjorie S. Cautley as affordable housing with private houses and co-op and rental apartment buildings, all arranged around parks and gardens on fifty-five acres and seventeen city blocks (see fig. 2.21). The six-story Phipps Garden Apartments complex, designed by Henry Wright, was added between 1931 and 1935. It was anticipated that the Aluminaire House would join the legacy of these important contributions to the modern apartment and residential community designs developed in New York City in the early part of the twentieth century. The site seemed appropriate for the house and the house seemed appropriate for the site.

Two apartment buildings, containing eight residential units, were designed by Campani and Schwarting Architects to make a suitable spatial backdrop for the Aluminaire House in massing, scale, and appearance. The design was contemporary, with a pattern of openings and wall surface to create a complexity that would set off the simplicity of the Aluminaire House while fitting with the articulated masonry surfaces of the Sunnyside Gardens and Phipps buildings. Brick-colored terra-cotta panels had been selected to mediate with the aluminum panels of the Aluminaire House and the predominantly masonry context. The units were designed with stoops to provide a ground-level residential scale matching that prominently found in the Sunnyside neighborhood. Upper terraces related to both the Aluminaire House and the corner units of the Sunnyside Gardens residences.

OPPOSITE

Figure 4.47 Existing and proposed site plan and isometric view.

Figure 4.48 Elevations of the house and its context, with plans of the Aluminaire House and proposed apartments.

Figure 4.49 View from the corner.

Once completed, the Aluminaire House was to be reinstated on the National Register and become a museum, open to the public. The garage was to be used in the same way that Le Corbusier added a diorama of his "City of Tomorrow" in the 1925 Esprit Nouveau Pavilion, to exhibit the real meaning of the house. It was to provide the history of the search for ways to create affordable housing and would include the display and information of the Sunnyside Gardens housing and Phipps Garden Apartments, as well as Aluminaire.

The apartment buildings were redesigned based on comments from the LPC and the design was simplified to be less prominent and more homogeneous with the adjacent Sunnyside Gardens context (see figs. 4.47–4.50).

BOTH IMAGES: Figure 4.50 Views from the streets.

Staff members at the New York City Landmarks Commission were enthusiastic about the project. The siting of the Aluminaire House in the context of Sunnyside was also supported by a number of preservationists, historians, and architects—Andrew Dolcart, Marta Gutman, Kenneth Frampton, and the Municipal Art Society—and support letters were offered by many prominent New York City architects.

Among the residents of Sunnyside there was support for the project from a small group of architects. However, most of the Sunnyside Gardens Association opposed the project. Community board meetings in Queens, and ultimately the hearing at the Landmarks Commission meeting in lower Manhattan, were well attended by Sunnyside residents, vocal in their opposition to the project, and local politicians, eager to please their constituents.

The NYC Landmarks Commission declined to approve the project in early 2014.

We were invited to lecture on the Aluminaire House at Modernism Week, Palm Springs, California, in February 2014. This was just after the Landmarks Commission decision not to approve the proposed site for the house in Sunnyside, Queens, New York.

5

PALM SPRINGS 2014–2024

TOP: **Figure 5.1** Frey House II, 1963–1964, San Jacinto Mountain, Palm Springs.

BOTTOM: **Figure 5.2** The Aluminaire House Foundation and the California Committee.

In the autumn of 2013, while the Aluminaire House Foundation was waiting for the New York City Landmarks Commission hearing and decision on the Sunnyside site proposal, we were invited to give a lecture/presentation on the Aluminaire House at the February 2014 Modernism Week events in Palm Springs, California. Mark Davis, then treasurer of Modernism Week and the primary organizer of events, extended the invitation. He also suggested that Palm Springs could provide a new site for the house. At the time, the Aluminaire House Foundation believed that the Sunnyside proposal would succeed, so we did not encourage speculation about moving the project to Palm Springs. But the lecture invitation was accepted.

On February 19, 2014, we gave that lecture on the Aluminaire House at the annual Modernism Week events at the Palm Springs Art Museum (PSAM) Annenberg Auditorium to a full-house audience. By that time, the NYC Landmarks Commission had voted against approval of the Sunnyside site proposal.

It was clear that this audience knew about, and were fond of, Albert Frey and his work. Frey had even willed his Frey House II to the museum. It was built in the San Jacinto Mountains just behind the museum in 1963–64, and visits were (and still are) conducted there during Modernism Week (see fig. 5.1). We gave an hour-long lecture, presenting the history of the house from its beginning in 1931 and our involvement with the house from 1987 up to the plans for it at the site in Sunnyside Gardens. At the end of the lecture the audience learned the NYC Landmarks Commission had not approved the project for Sunnyside Gardens. There was an extensive Q&A session, and one question was posed as to what the Foundation was going to do next with the house. When we answered that the Foundation had to look for new alternatives, someone asked if we would consider bringing it to Palm Springs, and there was a long and loud ovation. With this kind of enthusiasm, we knew this needed to be considered seriously.

Thus began a new, and thankfully final chapter to the eighty-three-year saga. However, little did we know that it would be another nine years until the groundbreaking for its reconstruction. An Aluminaire House California Committee was formed that included Mark Davis, Beth Edwards Harris, Tracy Conrad, Brad Dunning, and William Kopelk[1] (see fig. 5.2). An agreement was drawn up in 2014 that the California Committee would work with the Aluminaire House Foundation, a 501(c)(3) nonprofit, to do a feasibility study, leading to a final agreement that the California Committee would "transport, assemble, provide a permanent location and ongoing maintenance" of the house.

After the 2014 lecture in Palm Springs, we were invited back for other Modernism Week lectures in 2015, 2016, 2017, and 2018 to keep the excitement of its possible location there brewing. The February 17, 2017, lecture included a discussion with Susan Stamberg from National Public Radio (see fig. 5.3). The February 23, 2018, presentation included a clip from Philip Johnson's visit to the house in 1993 to celebrate its sixty-year birthday (two years late) and architectural historian Alan Hess moderated the Q&A. At the 2018 Modernism Week, money was donated to have an Aluminaire House–size scaffold and scrim with information on the Aluminaire House erected at the Modernism Week camp tent (headquarters) across the street, in front of the Palm Springs Museum of Art (see figs. 5.4 and 5.5). It was a beautiful object, particularly when lit at night. Being the exact size of the Aluminaire, it gave everyone in Palm Springs the opportunity to know its scale. Scheduled with these presentations were fundraisers organized by the California Committee to generate the construction funds.

TOP: Figure 5.3 Modernism Week lecture and discussion with Susan Stamberg, National Public Radio, February 2017.

CENTER: Figure 5.4 The Aluminaire "Cube" scrim on scaffold structure, Modernism Week, February 2018.

BOTTOM: Figure 5.5 Aluminaire "Cube" at night.

MOVING TO CALIFORNIA

In the winter of 2017, Mark Davis discussed moving the house in its trailer to Palm Springs. A city-owned site across from the museum had been proposed, and it seemed like the project might happen. Davis had an agreement drawn up in March 2017, permitting the California Committee to hire a semi-trailer truck driver to move the house in its trailer to a municipal storage lot in Palm Springs. The agreement stated that if the house was not reconstructed in Palm Springs, it would be returned to New York.

On February 8, 2017, the trailer that had contained the Aluminaire House since 2012 left the Cassone Trailer and Container Company yard in Ronkonkoma, Long Island, where it had been secretly parked for five years, for Palm Springs (see figs. 5.6 and 5.7). Mark Davis had an idea to vinyl wrap the trailer with images related to its contents. The wrap was designed by Gary Wexler and included large images of Albert Frey, the Harrison house of 1932, and Campani and Schwarting Architects' 3D drawings of the house. We arrived early in the morning to say goodbye on that cold February day. This was the first we had learned of its undisclosed location. The driver took pictures as it went out on its westward trip (see figs. 5.8–5.10).

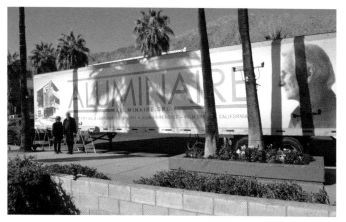

THE CALIFORNIA CONNECTION

After the Aluminaire project in 1931, Frey had worked with Kocher on a few projects in and around New York City. One of particular note was a weekend house in 1934 for Kocher near Northport on Long Island. Known also as the Experimental Weekend House or the "canvas house," it was a thirty-by-twenty-six-foot, open-plan, raised one-story structure, above ground on six round columns (like the Aluminaire House), with a terrace on the roof. It was sheathed in canvas, and clearly related to the Aluminaire in its style. It survived an intense hurricane in 1938 but was demolished for development in the 1950s (see figs. 1.57 and 1.58).

In 1934–35 Kocher and Frey also designed and built the Kocher-Samson Building in Palm Springs, the office and house for Dr. J. J. Kocher, brother of Lawrence Kocher (see fig. 5.13). Frey made a trip across the country to organize its construction in the small desert town of Palm Springs, California, surrounded by mountains. After seeing this project through, he went back to New York in 1937, and it seemed like he was establishing an interesting career as he worked with Philip

L. Goodwin and Edward Durell Stone on the construction of the Museum of Modern Art. (Frey had worked part time for William Lescaze in 1931–2 on designs for the MoMA.) But he was drawn back to Palm Springs in 1939, possibly by the mountains and perhaps by the way of life that was radically different from New York City. He established a successful architectural career and remained there the rest of his life.

Palm Springs, California, is not exactly a good place to locate this metal house, as Albert Frey told us in 1994, when we visited him for three days. He said he would never design such a thing in this climate. Palm Springs is one of nine oasis towns in the Coachella Valley, formed by the San Jacinto and Santa Rosa mountains and has a hot, dry desert climate. In the desert he radically changed his style of working from the Corbusian influences to a more Miesien style; from the cubic, subtractive strategy of the Aluminaire to the use of planes as X, Y, Z coordinates, more in keeping with neoplasticism (see fig. 5.16). This change may have been influenced by the Brick Wall House or the Barcelona Pavilion of Mies van der Rohe (see figs. 5.15 and 2.4). Frey himself has said that it came from a visit to Piet Mondrian's studio in 1933[2] (see fig. 5.17). He also noted that it was a more logical way of dealing with the sun and a desert climate in his later work[3] (see figs. 5.18–5.20). The more open, free plan with overhanging flat roofs, which Richard Neutra and Rudolf Schindler had also adopted in California, was much more suited to the climate, and Frey had no trouble adapting to this alternate way of building. Frey's work in Palm Springs was mainly residential, with the early Frey House I, and the later II, being the epitome of the evolution of this body of desert work (see figs. 5.14 and 5.1).

So, although the Aluminaire House does not fit well in the desert, its placement there does present the transformation that Albert Frey went through from his early career to the end of it, and, as such, Palm Springs has now become the showcase for the lifetime work of a prominent modern architect. The Aluminaire House Foundation felt that, despite the issues of climate and context, this was a good solution for the house.

TOP: **Figure 5.13** Kocher-Samson Building, Palm Springs, 1934–1935.
BOTTOM: **Figure 5.14** Frey House I, Palm Springs, 1940.

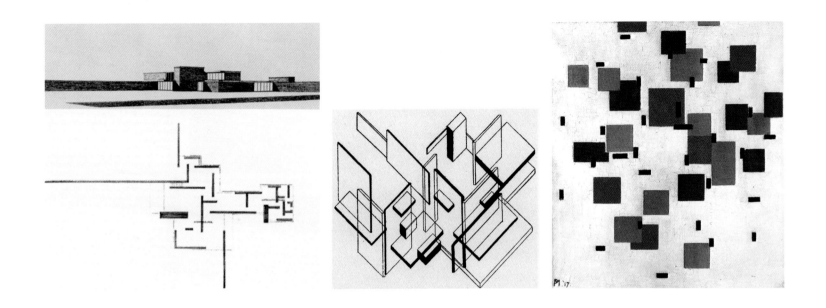

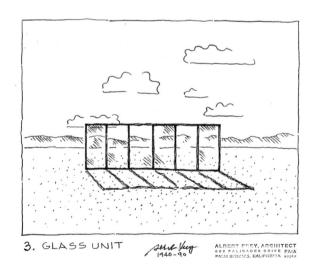

1. FLOOR SLAB

ALBERT FREY, ARCHITECT
690 PALISADES DRIVE FAIA
PALM SPRINGS, CALIFORNIA 92262

2. WALL UNIT

ALBERT FREY, ARCHITECT
690 PALISADES DRIVE FAIA
PALM SPRINGS, CALIFORNIA 92262

3. GLASS UNIT

ALBERT FREY, ARCHITECT
690 PALISADES DRIVE FAIA
PALM SPRINGS, CALIFORNIA 92262

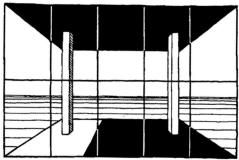

UPPER ROW, LEFT TO RIGHT

Figure 5.15 Mies van der Rohe "Brick Country House," 1923.

Figure 5.16 Theo van Doesburg and C. van Esteren, "Contra Constructie," 1923.

Figure 5.17 "Composition in Blue A," Piet Mondrian, 1917.

Figure 5.18 Albert Frey wrote in his *In Search of a Living Architecture*, "The confined shade emphasizes the sheltered space against the immensity of the out-of-doors."

Figure 5.19 Albert Frey wrote, "The sheltered area includes the space to distant horizons."

4. ROOF UNIT

ALBERT FREY, ARCHITECT
686 PALISADES DRIVE FAIA
PALM SPRINGS, CALIFORNIA 92262

5. COMPOSITION

ALBERT FREY, ARCHITECT
686 PALISADES DRIVE FAIA
PALM SPRINGS, CALIFORNIA 92262

Figure 5.20 Sequence: Floor, wall, glass roof, and composition sketches of the elements, Albert Frey.

SEARCHING FOR A SITE

The Aluminaire House Foundation and the California Committee considered a number of potential sites for the house but ran into difficulties in negotiations with each. We looked at placing it adjacent to the Design Center (see fig. 5.21), on the two vacant lots across the street from the museum that were owned by the City of Palm Springs that had parking below (see fig. 5.22). We also worked to integrate it into the public park that presently exists in front of the museum (see fig. 5.23). Even the idea of putting it inside the museum, or in one of its outdoor sunken sculpture gardens, was examined. Finally, on February 21, 2020, simultaneous offers were made by the California College of the Desert, which was about to build a new campus with a school of architecture in Palm Springs, and the Palm Springs Art Museum. We made presentations and had discussions with each. We quickly decided that PSAM was preferable, feeling that the cultural setting and public character of the site and institution would be most appropriate. The Aluminaire House had started as an exhibition and would end as an exhibition. An agreement for the Aluminaire House Foundation to give the house to the Palm Springs Museum was signed on July 7, 2020, by then-director Louis Grachos. An agreement for Campani and Schwarting Architects to be the architects for the reconstruction was also made with the museum.

Figure 5.21 Aluminaire House site study at the PSAM Design Center, Palm Springs.

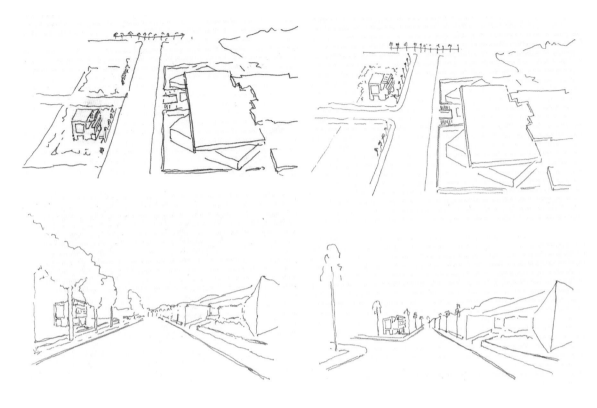

Figure 5.22 Site plan studies for city property over parking garages in front of the Palm Springs Art Museum.

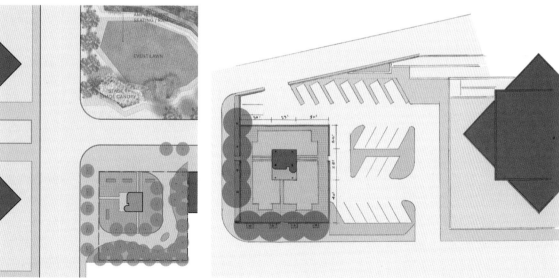

LEFT: Figure 5.23 Site plan study with sculpture garden integrated into the public park design, February 2018.

RIGHT: Figure 5.24 Campani and Schwarting Architects, site plan study to place the Aluminaire House at the south end of the PSAM parking lot, at the corner of Museum Drive and Tahquitz Canyon Way, with which Albert Frey aligned his Frey House II.

AN EXHIBITION PAVILION AT THE PALM SPRINGS ART MUSEUM

The Palm Springs Art Museum is an important cultural center in the city of Palm Springs and for the entire Coachella Valley of the Sonoran Desert. It was founded in 1938 as the Palm Springs Desert Museum and made several moves in the downtown area. The present building was built in 1974, and was designed by well-known local architect E. Stewart Williams.[4] It is interesting to note that Albert Frey had hoped to have that commission. The building is in an important urban location just blocks from Palm Canyon Drive, the main north-south street, and at the end of West Tahquitz Canyon Way, the primary east-west street that terminates in the east at the airport and at the San Jacinto Mountains

to the west, where Albert Frey designed and built his second house, Frey House II, and where he lived from its completion in 1964 until his death in 1998. The museum was sited at the base of these mountains, so it is in the enviable situation of being in the center of downtown Palm Springs yet set against a mountain with hiking trails originating at its site. The Williams design is quite monumental for a modern building, with bilateral symmetry, a central entrance, a lobby, and its largest gallery (an enclosed space that was originally a sculpture court) on the central axis. Flanking the central cubic form are cantilevered diagonal galleries that hover above suppressed sculpture gardens (see fig. 5.25). There

Figure 5.25 The Palm Springs Art Museum with Aluminaire frame at left.

are off-street parking areas on the north and south sides of the building. A portion of the smaller lot to the south, extending to West Tahquitz Canyon Way, was designated as the site for the Aluminaire House. It would be easily accessible as part of the museum's permanent collection, but also visible on its own as part of the downtown scene. Sitting on a corner site of two main streets, the house would be able to present its two most notable sides: the front façade facing Museum Drive, like the museum itself, and the characteristic façade with the double-story living room window facing Tahquitz Canyon Way (see figs. 5.24 and 5.26). The site provides an excellent exposure of the house to the city.

After changes in the museum administration, and the COVID-19 pandemic delay experienced by so many projects globally, in June 2023 the museum embarked on the reconstruction. The California Committee's involvement gave way to the museum's project committee of trustees, who formed a design committee and organized regular weekly owner/architect/contractor meetings to follow through on the construction of the house. The primary representatives for the museum were trustee Leo Marmol, principal of Marmol Radzner of Los Angeles with a portfolio of significant midcentury modern architecture restorations, trustee L. J. Cella, and director Adam Lerner.

The Palm Springs Art Museum contracted Campani and Schwarting Architects as the "historical architects" to assist with preservation issues during the reconstruction, while Allen Sanborn, a local architect, was contracted as the executive architect to file the project with the building department, obtain the building permit, and deal with the issues of day-to-day construction. Many of our drawings that were made in the 1990s for the Historical Structures Report were adopted into the construction documents. Other firms were contracted to do structural engineering, site engineering, landscape design, and mechanical, electrical, and plumbing engineering. DW Johnston was contracted for the construction. Our task was to comment on and answer questions related to the historical accuracy of the reconstruction. As we had been involved in the house for thirty-seven years, deconstructing it twice and constructing much of it once, we had the experience and knowledge of how to build the house to contribute to the project.

Figure 5.26 Site plan study at PSAM, renderings presented to the museum.

THE THIRD RECONSTRUCTION, 2023–2024

After getting the building permit, determining costs, and conducting fundraising to cover those costs, construction was started in July 2023. The structural erection and the cladding of the house with the panels were our first two visits to the site. Two more visits were made as the construction continued to completion in February 2024.

There was a lot of discussion about the siting, orientation, and landscaping of the house at the museum. There were some who wanted the house landscaped as a single-family residential context, but we were firm that the house was originally, and was to become, an exhibition pavilion. Most important, we felt it critical to convey Kocher and Frey's ideas about creating multiples of the house that could be organized into low-rise, high-density, residential urban blocks. In addition, because the house would never have been designed for the desert, a logical decision in favor of simplification and abstraction of the landscape prevailed. In 2020, when we donated the house to the museum, we had presented a site plan and simple renderings of the house on the site where it was to be built (see figs. 5.24 and 5.26). With this site and orientation, the construction of an aluminum building in the desert heat with the large window facing south needed to be reconciled with the landscaping.

Figure 5.27 Renderings of the Aluminaire House by the Palm Springs Art Museum.

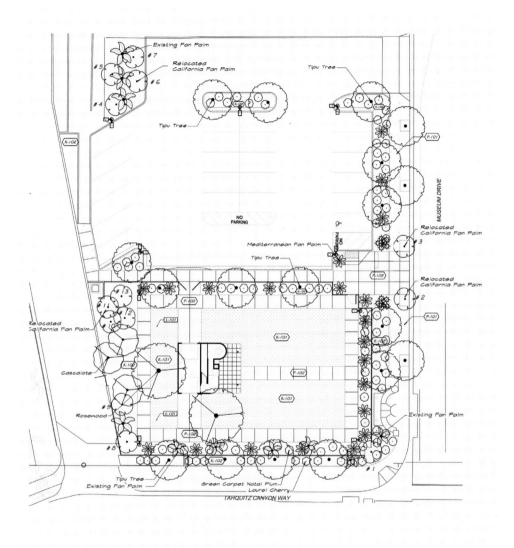

Figure 5.28 Final Landscape Plan by TKD Associates, Rancho Mirage, California, December 4, 2023.

There was fundamental original material that could still be reused, such as the aluminum and steel frame and steel windows, and the aluminum bathroom cabinet, but there was a large list of missing materials. The aluminum panels and metal floor decking had been replaced in the NYIT reconstruction and the panels and some decking would have to be replaced again. Other materials were simply missing altogether and had to be substituted. Fortunately, at the original Allied Arts and Industry exhibition in April 1931, a list of all the donated materials had been produced, titled "Companies and Manufacturers That Supplied Materials for the Exhibition House." This list also had a short description of each material, and this was used as a critical reference document for their replacement. In the 1980s, students who worked on the Aluminaire House researched these companies and materials and their work was also a resource for replacement. Some materials were easy to replace with the same or similar materials. For instance, the garage door company for the missing two doors still exists and makes the same product.

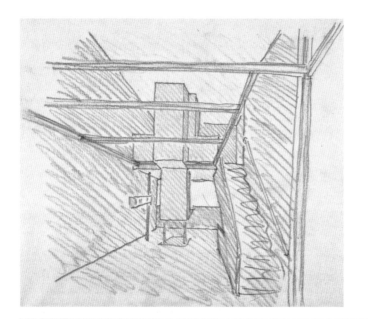

There were quite a few decisions to be made. One of the most complicated was how to adapt the house to meet seismic requirements. This was achieved, in part, by replacing the half-inch insulation board that was originally used in the wall construction with half-inch plywood as well as diagonal steel strapping that would solve "shear" (lateral movement) issues. A second complicated issue was how to meet heating, ventilation, and air-conditioning requirements. This was rather neatly resolved by utilizing the dumbwaiter shaft for the ductwork from the HVAC unit that was located in the closet under the stair. There were no roof drains in the 1931 exhibition. Albert Frey said that he didn't remember any lighting other than the cove lighting above the living room windows to simulate daylight, so this was a problem to solve. We suggested non-fixed lighting that would indicate that it was not part of the Frey design.

ABOVE: Figure 5.29 Albert Frey's study (before deciding on the glass case for the dining room) for the colors of the interior, pencil on paper.

LEFT: Figure 5.30 Fabrikoid, Muralart ad by DuPont, 1930s.

One very important issue was that we needed to communicate to the contractor how we had installed the aluminum panels. This began with our accepted recommendation that new panels be used even though the ones that were removed were all in the trailer. We had learned from experience that it was a delicate operation to set the panels properly and carefully screw them with the aluminum screws and washers. Power tools could not be used since the pressure had to be exact to not crimp the panels. We had used oversize holes to allow the panels to move as they expanded and contracted with temperature changes, which would be more dramatic in the desert climate.

Some critical materials were more difficult to replace. The most important of these is the wall covering that was selected for the exhibition. Kocher and Frey had selected a product by DuPont named Fabrikoid. There were different kinds of Fabrikoid that were to be used from automobile and train seats, furniture, luggage, and book covers to wall coverings (see fig. 5.30). The material for the Aluminaire wall covering was a type of Fabrikoid called Muralart. Muralart was described in DuPont advertisements as a pyroxylin coating solution on a woven cotton base—a semiliquid solution of nitrated cotton dissolved in solvents with patterns pressed into it.[5] We researched this material at the Hagely Museum and Library at the DuPont headquarters and factory in Wilmington, Delaware, and at the Frederick Schumacher and Company fabric company (founded in 1889 and located on Fifth Avenue in New York City) that supplied the Muralart for the project, but were unable to find any samples or color selections. From our research in 1995 at the Kocher Archive in Williamsburg, Virginia, we found a sketch perspective of the living/dining room made with color crayons (see fig. 5.29). It was an early design study; the glass case holding the roll-out table was not in the sketch so the Muralart may not yet have been chosen. However, this sketch does show Albert Frey's intentions, which are consistent with his later work. In 1994 Frey told us that the wall coverings were in pastel colors. He also mentioned being influenced by the early work of Le Corbusier. Le Corbusier's inclination to paint his projects with multiple colors is well known and published (see figs. 2.30 and 2.31).[6] We discovered that Schumacher could produce an acceptable replacement to the Fabrikoid. Since this would be a critical aspect of the interior experience we proposed to paint the walls the colors found in the single Frey sketch. This way the effects could be assessed before proceeding with a final fabric.

The construction went pretty much on schedule and budget and the project was completed in February 2024. The site is bound by a simple metal fence and has gray tone cement walkways and pewter gray crushed stone rock surrounding the house to complement the aluminum building (see 5.28). Renderings were created when the site plan was finalized to help visualize the outcome as the work proceeded (see fig. 5.27).

THE CONSTRUCTION IN PALM SPRINGS

OPPOSITE

UPPER LEFT: First the five-inch-diameter aluminum columns are set on their concrete footings.

UPPER RIGHT: The reinforcing in the foundation and slab for earthquake protection.

LOWER LEFT: The concrete slab reveals the plan.

LOWER RIGHT: Three stories of continuous aluminum columns and the cantilevered girders.

ABOVE

LEFT: The original aluminum structure and vertical steel girts that hold the façade.

CENTER: The frame.

RIGHT: The new aluminum panel façade against the mountain.

The formal front façade with columns, strip window, and lower and upper terraces.

The signature side façade with the double-height living room window wall and angled wall of the terrace above and the recessed entry terrace at ground level.

Side façade with dining room and kitchen windows.

Back façade. Albert Frey said another unit could be attached here.

An important view that reveals
the whole house.

A view that reveals the house's
solid and void character.

The dynamic side contrasting the static back.

A view into the living room and thus, into the house.

The garage below the living room.

The front entry terrace.

House with open windows.

FUTURE WORK

With all of this competed work, the Aluminaire House will still need to be finished on the inside. In addition to the saga over the Fabrikoid, bathroom fixtures, kitchen cabinets, and appliances from 1931 will have to be found. Frey's fixed furniture of cabinets, and most importantly, the roll-out dining table need to be reconstructed. Perhaps even the other furniture that Frey designed, such as the inflatable rubber living room chairs, the spring-like stool, and the bathroom chair with the "endless towel," will also be fabricated. The garage can be used as an exhibition space for artifacts of the original and information about the house that we have tried to provide in this book. The museum has discussed creating a virtual reality visit of the interior. Our hope is that the Palm Springs Building Department will give permission for the museum to conduct guided tour visits to the inside. So the story continues, but at this point we have done our job to save this valuable exhibition of what they proclaimed in 1931 to be the "House of the Future."

Front door entry with dumbwaiter at ground floor.

Entryway with column and stair to the second floor.

Entryway from stair.

UPPER LEFT: Dining and living room from stair to ground floor entryway.

LOWER LEFT: Dining room with kitchen door and stair to below and above.

UPPER RIGHT: Living room and dining room with stairs.

LOWER RIGHT: Living room with view into the bedroom.

TOP: View into dining room.

BOTTOM: View from dining room into living room.
The expandable table is missing.

OPPOSITE

LEFT: Column in living room.

RIGHT: View of the upper living room with window wall.

OPPOSITE

LEFT: Double-height living room and stair to the library.

RIGHT: Dining room and living room with the stair to the entry at ground floor.

LEFT: Bedroom with the window wall of the front façade, looking toward the unfinished bathroom.

RIGHT: View from the bathroom toward the bedroom.

View of the living room and window wall.

View of the window wall.

View from the living room to the dining room with stair to below and above.

Living room with bathroom above.

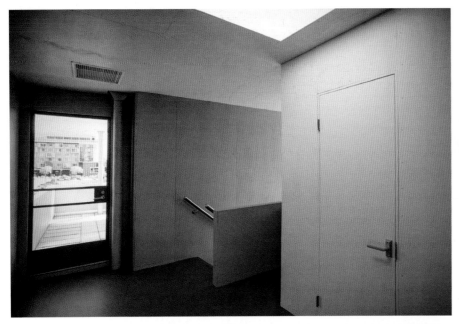

UPPER LEFT: View of the door to the terrace from the library and stair to the living room.

LOWER LEFT: View of the bathroom and upper living room from the library.

UPPER RIGHT: View on the terrace with the dumbwaiter and wall for a fold-down table (not yet built) and the aligned angled wall at the end of the terrace.

LOWER RIGHT: Terrace open above area and dumbwaiter volume.

View of the upper terrace.

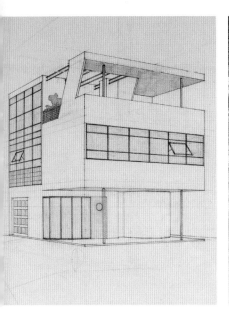

Conclusion

The Aluminaire House has been a big part of our lives for thirty-seven years. The resolution of its final destiny certainly took longer than we ever could have imagined and, also, longer than it should have. But it has been a great adventure with key chapters: saving and rebuilding the house with architecture students, visiting and interviewing Albert Frey, designing a context for it in Sunnyside Gardens. Then there was sending it off in its trailer from Long Island and seeing its arrival in Palm Springs. Finally, our gifting it to the Palm Springs Art Museum and being the historical architects for its third and final reconstruction. That has been a good ending. It started as an exhibition that we needed to research and imagine, and it has ended as an exhibition that we have had responsibilities for and finally got to see and experience. It was to be demolished when we started this saga, and now it is in good hands and in a good place. In the end, what pleases us most is that it lives on and so many other people will now get to experience it both as a phenomenon and hopefully also as an idea.

—Jon Michael Schwarting and Frances Campani

Acknowledgments

There are many people and institutions to thank for their help in the rescue, restoration, and reconstruction of the Aluminaire House, and ultimately the creation of this book on the house and its significance.

In 1986, Paul Goldberger and Joseph Rosa sounded the alarm on its imminent demolition. The New York Institute of Technology, under President Matthew Schure and Dean of Architecture Julio M. San Jose, supported Michael's proposal to take the house and the project on as part of the curriculum at the School of Architecture. NYIT students deserve enormous credit for working on the house with enthusiasm. New York State Department of Parks, Recreation, and Historic Preservation (then directed by Michael Lynch) funded the unusual preservation/reconstruction project. The Alcoa Foundation also supported the project financially and with technical assistance. Preservationist Elise Quasebarth of Higgins and Quasebarth wrote the Historic Structures report.

As the project continued, funds were raised by the "Friends of the Aluminaire House." The Kaplan Foundation awarded us a Furthermore Grant toward the text about the house.

The Aluminaire House Foundation, Inc., was formed with generous legal help from Charlie Russo of Russo, Karl, Widmaier, Cordano. Kenneth Frampton, Ware Professor of Architecture at Columbia GSAPP, gave important support to the project by serving on the Foundation's board.

We are grateful also to those who supported the Sunnyside site proposal. Many architects devoted time and professional testimony at the Landmarks Commission Hearing.

The move to Palm Springs was envisioned and spearheaded by Mark Davis. The California Committee—Mark Davis, William Kopelk, Beth Edwards Harris, Brad Dunning, and Tracy Conrad—was essential in the Palm Springs site search and in encouraging the project. We are also grateful to Palm Springs Art Museum directors Louis Grachos and Adam Lerner.

During the work by the Aluminaire House Foundation, Heather Korb, in the office of Campani and Schwarting Architects, was essential in helping produce the images to envision the house on various sites, and in providing assistance with this book.

The late Gibbs Smith took a special interest in the project. He was excited about the agenda of the Aluminaire exhibition house for affordable housing. We are grateful to him and all the staff at Gibbs Smith for this publication.

Most of all we want to thank Albert Frey. We are grateful to A. Lawrence Kocher for initiating the project. He hired Albert Frey and gave him responsibility for the design and credit for the Exhibition House. But we feel we were able to "meet" Albert Frey as we studied and understood the house. By the time we physically met him in 1994, we felt like we were old friends. He patiently and knowledgeably answered many questions that helped us in the reconstruction. Albert Frey's brilliant, significant Aluminaire House is the reason for this thirty-seven-year-long project.

Notes

1. THE ALUMINAIRE HOUSE—1931

1. Schwarting and Campani interview with Albert Frey, May 26, 27, and 28, 1994.
2. Schwarting and Campani interview, 1994.
3. Schwarting and Campani interview, 1994.
4. The Grand Central Palace was an exhibition hall built in 1911 and demolished in 1963. It was located at Lexington Avenue between 46th and 47th Streets. It was a 13-story, whole-block building with three floors of exhibition space. The central exhibition space was 48 feet high. See David W. Dunlap, "When Trade Shows Were Both Grand and Central," *New York Times,* December 18, 2012.
5. Alfred H. Barr, preface to *The International Style: Architecture Since 1922,* by Henry Russell Hitchcock and Phillip Johnson (New York: W. W. Norton & Company, 1966) 11.
6. Sweet's Catalog has been published from 1906 to today as a compilation of manufacturer's catalogs or literature.
7. Joseph Rosa, *Albert Frey, Architect* (New York: Rizzoli International, 1990). Rosa states, "Its actual size was dictated by the size of the exhibition space," and attributes this to the May 1932 issue of *Shelter.*
8. Le Corbusier made this concrete structural diagram for making repeatable interconnected housing units (like dominoes). The structural columns permitted walls to be placed freely for spatial or functional requirements. Albert Frey's diagram is a metal frame version of this idea.
9. Philip Johnson, "Rejected Architects," *Creative Art* 8, no. 6 (June 1931): 433–35.
10. Advertisement, *Brooklyn Daily Eagle,* April 17, 1931.
11. John J. O'Neil, "Illuminated Windows in the House of Future," *Brooklyn Daily Eagle,* April 18, 1931.
12. Lloyd Jacquet, "Aluminum House at Architects' Show Marks New Building Era," *New York Herald Tribune,* April 19, 1931.
13. "Architectural Art Is Exhibited Here," *New York Times,* April 19, 1931.
14. "Architects' Show Visited by 100,000," *New York Times,* April 26, 1931.
15. Jean Lyon, "Housewife May Soon Order More Rooms by Telephone and Delivered by Parcel Post—Kitchen of the Future," *New York Sun,* April 23, 1931.
16. Logan U. Reaves, "Cut-Away Representation of the Home of the Future," *Popular Mechanics,* September 1932.
17. Buckminster Fuller, ed., *Shelter—A Correlating Medium for the Forces of Architecture* 2, no. 4 (May 1932). Buckminster Fuller was the pro-tem editor of this edition. *Shelter* was a journal published from 1932 to 1939. The 1939 issue stated that it was by a progressive group of architects devoted to "achieving an adequate public housing program for the American people."
18. DuPont described it as a Nitrocellulose "Proxlin spread on cotton . . . a semi-liquid of nitrated cotton dissolved in solvents . . . applied to the cotton in thin layers until the desired weight is attained . . . embossed or pressed under heat and pressure." Hagley.org.
19. There was no evidence of this in 1987.
20. Kocher and Frey published an article on closet planning in *Architectural Record* (March 1931).
21. Curiously, there is the possibility to have had windows to the terrace bring in light and make a visual relationship between inside and outside, but there are none. This was done similarly in Le Corbusier's Esprit Nouveau pavilion between the living room and terrace.
22. Charlotte Perriand designed a roll-out table that was built for her own apartment. This was an obvious influence on Albert Frey.
23. A drawing by Albert Frey was made for a stair connecting a mezzanine and the floor and door to be cut into the second floor of the back façade (Colonial Williamsburg-Rockefeller Library Collection).
24. A biographical note on Kocher can be found in the Colonial Williamsburg- Rockefeller Library Collection, https://research.colonial Williamsburg.org–A. Lawrence Kocher.
25. Lawrence A. Kocher obituary, *New York Times,* June 15, 1969.
26. Suzanne Stephens, "Lawrence Kocher, Renaissance Man," *Architectural Record,* April 1, 2016. https://www.architecturalrecord.com/articles/11585-lawrence-kocher-renaissance-man.
27. Rosa, *Albert Frey,* 12.
28. Schwarting and Campani interview with Frey, May 1994.
29. The Maisons Loucheur project was for housing after WWI. Its square plan had a day and night arrangement. They were two-family, back-to-back units with zinc panels. The Aluminaire House has a blank back, suggesting the possibility of putting them back-to-back, Albert Frey told Schwarting and Campani.
30. Kocher suggested the full-scale house in September 1930 (Rosa, 27).
31. Albert Frey, *In Search of a Living Architecture* (New York: Architectural Book Publishing Company, 1939).

2. CONTEXT AND ISSUES

1. Lewis Mumford, "Mass Production and the Modern House," *Architectural Record* 67, no. 1 (January 1930): 13–20, and 67, no. 2 (February 1930): 110–116.
2. A. Lawrence Kocher and Albert Frey, "The Real Estate Subdivisions for Low Cost Housing," *Architectural Record,* April 1931, 323–27, the same month as the Aluminaire House publication.
3. Douglas Haskell, "The Architectural League and the Rejected Architects," *Parnassus* 3, no. 5 (May 1931): 12–13.
4. Catherine K. Bauer, "Who Cares About Architecture?" *The New Republic* 66 (May 5, 1931): 326–27.
5. Haskell, "The Architectural League." pages 12–13.
6. Haskell, pages 12-13.
7. Bauer, 327.
8. Douglas Haskell, "The House of the Future," *The New Republic* 66 (May 13, 1931): 344–45.
9. Lewis Mumford, "The Flaw of the Mechanical House," *The New Republic* (June 5, 1931): 65–66.
10. "A Communication—Mr. Mumford, Mr. Haskell and the Factory-built House," *The New Republic* (July 1, 1931): 180–81 and Lewis Mumford, "A Communication—What Prevents Good Housing?", *The New Republic* (July 8, 1931): 208–10.
11. Philip Johnson, *Mies van der Rohe* (New York: The Museum of Modern Art, 1947), 184.
12. Johnson, *Mies,* 183.
13. Johnson, 190.
14. Johnson, 184.
15. Le Corbusier, *Towards a New Architecture,* repr. ed. (London: Architectural Press, 1959), 12.
16. Alberto Sartoris, *Gli Elementi dell' Architettura Funzionale* (Milan: Ulrico Hoepli, 1940).
17. F. R. S. Yorke, *The Modern House* (London: Architectural Press, 1934).
18. Colin Rowe, "The Chicago Frame; Chicago's Place in the Modern Movement," *Architectural Review* 120 (November 1956): 285–89.

19. See Richard Plunz, *A History of Housing in New York City* (New York: Columbia University Press, 1992). There is also the work on block formations of Henry Wright and Clarence Stein and realized in Sunnyside Gardens in Queens, New York, as did Kocher and Frey in their *Architectural Record* article.
20. Le Corbusier published a book titled *Une Maison-Un Palais* (Paris: Cres & Cie, 1928). The implication is that modern architects were now interested in the working class rather than the aristocracy

3. THE HARRISON HOUSE—1932

1. Victoria Newhouse, *Wallace K. Harrison, Architect* (New York: Rizzoli International, 1989). Newhouse provides a thorough biography of Harrison.
2. Newhouse, *Wallace K. Harrison*, 60.
3. Newhouse, *Wallace K. Harrison*, 28–29.
4. Schwarting and Campani interview with Albert Frey, May 1994.
5. Newhouse, 60.
6. "Architect to Erect Glass Home for Self," *Brooklyn Daily Eagle*, June 21, 1931.
7. Newhouse, 60. In the NYIT reconstruction, the wood nailers were found screwed to the steel angle girts. Some wood plugs were found unused in the steel girts.
8. Joseph Rosa, *Albert Frey, Architect* (New York: Rizzoli International, 1990), 28, and Schwarting and Campani interview,1994.
9. J. P. Lohman, "Modern Home Built of Glass and Aluminum," *New York American*, December 6, 1931, 1–2.
10. Lohman, "Modern Home."
11. Lohman, "Modern Home."
12. Newhouse, 60. Harrison married Ellen Milton, whose brother married John D. Rockefeller Jr.'s only daughter, Abby. Harrison began working for John D. Rockefeller Jr. on Rockefeller Center in 1928 and designed Nelson Rockefeller's apartment in 1930.
13. Henry-Russell Hitchcock, Jr. and Philip Johnson, *The International Style: Architecture Since 1922* (New York: W. W. Norton, 1932), 39.
14. Hitchcock and Johnson, *The International Style*, 80–81.
15. Hitchcock and Johnson, 94.

4. THE HOUSE 1932–2014

1. *Life,* April 1935.
2. The plan of the house, as described by Hester Diamond (second owner of the house) for Harrison's biographer, Victoria Newhouse, can be seen in fig. 3.14. The authors have located the Aluminaire House within the 2009 restoration plans of the Harrison house by architects Schappacher White of NYC (fig. 3.13). One can locate the Aluminaire House being moved about 150 feet in the demolition plan filed with the Town of Huntington, Long Island (fig. 3.15).
3. A signed and dated insulation panel was present from the 1931–32 reconstruction as well as some pre-1940 wiring.
4. F. R. S. Yorke, *The Modern House* (London: Architectural Press, 1934).
5. Hester Diamond was an art dealer in New York City who bought the house after Harrison's passing. She sold the Leger drawing in the circular living room to the Cologne Museum in Germany when she sold the house in the 1980s.
6. The whole site was designated so the Aluminaire House was included in the designation. It was taken off the Register when the house was removed from the site. It was also on the New York State Register of Historic Places. A Building-Structure Inventory Form by the Division for Historic Preservation, New York State Parks and Recreation, listed Harold Diamond as the present owner and listed "aluminum pre-fab house," but that was dropped because the House was no longer in New York.
7. This became Joseph Rosa's book *Albert Frey, Architect* (New York: Rizzoli International, 1990).
8. Michael Lynch continued to be involved with the project, even supporting its move to Sunnyside Gardens with a New York City Landmarks Preservation Commission presentation.
9. The use of a forced air system is noted in F. R. S. Yorke's book but there is no accommodation for the requisite ductwork. However, to meet California codes, a heating and air-conditioning system is in the Palm Springs Art Museum reconstruction.
10. The Alcoa Foundation gave a grant of $10,000 to the project.
11. "The Aluminaire House—Historic Structures Report" was completed in January 1996 by Higgin & Quasebarth, New York, New York, with contributions from Andrew Dolkart, architectural historian, and New York Institute of Technology professor Jon Michael Schwarting and assistant professor Frances Campani.

5. PALM SPRINGS 2014–2024

1. L. to R.: Beth Edwards is an architectural historian, critic, researcher, and writer—she is the former owner and restorer of the Richard Neutra Kaufmann House in Palm Springs; Frances Campani; William Kopelk is a landscape architect—he cofounded Modernism Week in Palm Springs in 2005 and is presently chairman of the board of directors of Modernism Week; Tracy Conrad is president of the Palm Springs Historical Society and CEO of the Smoke Tree Ranch compound; Mark Davis is on the board of directors of Modernism Week and is its treasurer—he has been a critical planner and organizer of Modernism Week for 13 years; Jon Michael Schwarting. Brad Dunning of Brad Dunning Design (not pictured) was briefly a member of the committee. He is the curator of the Albert Frey exhibition at the Palm Springs Art Museum that started January 2024.
2. Joseph Rosa, *Albert Frey, Architect* (New York: Rizzoli, 1990), 33, and Schwarting and Campani interview with Albert Frey, 1994.
3. Albert Frey, *In Search of a Living Architecture* (New York: Architectural Book Publishing Company, 1939), 68.
4. E. Stewart Williams (1909–2005) was an important midcentury modern architect who started a practice in Palm Springs in 1946. His success began with the Frank Sinatra house in 1947. He designed the Santa Fe Federal Savings and Loan Association in 1960, which is now the Palm Springs Art Museum Architecture and Design Center. He designed the Palm Springs Art Museum, which was completed in 1976.
5. When we researched the Hagley Museum and Library in Wilmington, Delaware, we were not able to find information or samples of the wallcovering material or colors. We also researched the Schumacher archive in Brooklyn, New York, but were unsuccessful. We concluded that there was no evidence of the original Fabrikoid material or colors that Albert Frey selected. However, Schumacher continues to distribute wall coverings that continue their line going back in time. They also now have the technology to match any color. Using the color drawing of Albert Frey (see fig. 1.21), which was done with crayons, we presented a proposed color palate to the Palm Springs Art Museum in August 2023 that was approved.
6. Couleurs Suisse Ag have researched and offered "Les Couleurs Le Corbusier" paints. There are 43 "colour palette of 1931" and 20 "colour palette of 1959." Le Corbusier frequently used different colors on different walls of the same room. Frey was obviously aware of this and influenced by it. His palette later evolved in relation to the colors of the desert, but his color schemes of using different colors in the same space continued.

Illustration and Photography Credits

Note: Diligent effort has been made to ascertain original photographers or copyright holders; in a few instances, the trail ended without conclusion. To provide information that might enlighten photo credits for future printings, please contact the authors or publisher.

*The photo research for copyrights to these images resulted in a dead end. The images appear in numerous books that are copyrighted but the images are not. We have not been able to locate the original source, which dates back 85 to 95 years.

—Jon Michael Schwarting and Frances Campani

A. Lawrence Kocher and Albert Frey, "The Real Estate Subdivisions for Low Cost Housing," © *Architectural Record*, BNP Media, April 1931, 323–27: Figures 2.2, 2.3

Architecture and Design Collection, Art, Design, & Architecture Museum, University of California Santa Barbara: Figures 5.13, 5.14

Albert Frey: Figures 1.44 and 5.20

*Albert Frey, *In Search of a Living Architecture* (New York: Architectural Book Publishing Company, 1939): Figures 5.18, 5.19

"Aluminaire: A House for Contemporary Life," *Shelter*, 2 (May 1932): Figures 1.6, 1.7

"Architects' Show Visited by 100,000," *New York Times*, April 26, 1931: Figure 1.9

Brooklyn Daily Eagle, April 17, 1931: Figure 0.1

*Christian Hubert and Lindsay Stamm Shapiro, *William Lescaze* (New York: Institute for Architecture and Urban Studies and Rizzoli International, 1982): Figure 2.12

Stein, Clarence S. introduction by Lewis Mumford, *Toward New Towns for America*, Fig. 3 (p 23) Sunnyside Gardens site plan, © 1966 Clarence S. Stein, by permission of The MIT Press: Figure 2.21

Colin Rowe, "Chicago Frame: Chicago's Place in the Modern Movement," *Architectural Review* 120, no. 718 (November 1956): 285–289: Figure 2.8

Dan Chavkin: All photographs pages 144–150, 152–161

DW Johnston Construction: Photographs page 143, left and center

*Esther McCoy, *Richard Neutra*, Masters of Architecture (New York: George Braziller, 1960): Figures 2.10, 2.11

*F.R.S. Yorke, *The Modern House* (London: Architectural Press, 1934): Figure 1.13

Fabrikoid advertisement circa the 1930s: Figures 1.14, 5.30

© FLC / ADAGP, Paris / Artists Rights Society (ARS) New York 2024: Figures 2.30, 2.31

Guillaume Goureau, Palm Springs Art Museum: Photographs page 151, page 162 far right, page 168

Hans L. C. Jaffe, *De Stijl* (New York: Harry N. Abrams, 1971): Figure 5.16

Harrison House renovation plan, collaged with Aluminaire House, on plan by Schappacher White Architects, New York, 2006: Figure 3.13

*Henry Russell Hitchcock and Philip Johnson, *The International Style; Architecture Since 1922* (W. W. Norton & Company, 1966): Figures 1.45, 2.13, 3.16

James Marston Fitch, *Walter Gropius* (New York: George Braziller, 1960): Figure 2.6

Jeff Durkin, Breadtruck Films: Figure 5.11

Jon Michael Schwarting and Frances Campani: Figures 1.31, 1.41, 1.42, 2.32, 4.1–4.50, 5.4–5.7, 5.21– 5.26, all photos on page 142, far right photograph on page 143, center right photograph on page 162

Jon Michael Schwarting, "Aluminaire Update," *Podium*, American Institute of Architects, Long Island Chapter, summer 1989, 5–8: Figure 2.32

Landscape Plan by TKD Associates, Rancho Mirage, California, August 11, 2023: Figure 5.28

Special Collections, John D. Rockefeller Jr. Library, The Colonial Williamsburg Foundation, Williamsburg, VA: Figures 0.2, 1.1, 1.2, 1.4, 1.5,1.12,1.15–1.30, 1.32–1.39, 1.59, 3.2–3.11, 5.29, far left and center left on page 162

*Le Corbusier and Pierre Jeanneret, *Oeuvre Complete 1929–1934*, (Erlenbach-Zurich: Les Editions d'Architecture, 1947): Figure 1.49

*Le Corbusier, Pierre Jeanneret, and Willy Boesinger, *Oeuvre Complete 1910–1929*, 7th ed. (Zurich: Les Editions Girsberger-Zurich, 1960): Figures 1.40,1.46–1.48, 1.50- 1.51, 2.5, 2.26–2.29

*Leonardo Benevolo, *History of Modern Architecture*, vol. 2, *The Modern Movement* (Cambridge, MA: MIT Press, 1971): Figures 2.7, 2.15–2.19, 2.23, 2.24

Library of Congress, Historic American Buildings Survey: Figure 2.9

Life magazine, April 1935: Figure 3.12

Logan U. Reaves, "Cut-Away Representation of the Home of the Future," *Popular Mechanics*, September 1932: Figure 1.11

Mark Davis, Modernism Week, Palm Springs: Figures 5.2, 5.3, 5.12

New York Herald Tribune, April 19, 1931: Figure 1.10

Courtesy of Palm Springs Art Museum, Albert Frey Collection
55-1999.2: Figures 1.52–1.58, 2.1

Courtesy of Palm Springs Art Museum, Renderings Claudiu
Cengher: Figure 5.27

Palm Springs Bureau of Tourism: Figure 5.1

Philip Johnson, *Mies van der Rohe*, 1947, Digital Image ©
The Museum of Modern Art, Licensed by SCALA / Art
Resource, NY: Figures 2.4, 2.14, 5.15

Piet Mondrian, *Composition in Blue B*, 1917, oil on canvas,
50.3 x 45.3 cm, Kroller-Muller Museum, Ontario, Canada:
Figure 5.17

Popular Science, July 1931: Figure 1.8

Postcard: Figure 1.3

R. Buckminster Fuller, *Ideas and Integrities* (Collier Books,
1963) Lib. Congress cat card # 63-11571: Figure 2.25

Ricardo Gonzales: Figures 5.8–5.10

Romerstadt photo by May and Wichert, 1930, digitized by
Heidelberg University Library, CC-BY-SA3.0: Figure 2.22

"The Architecture of Black Mountain College," Mondo Blogo,
December 28, 2010 http://mondo-blogo.blogspot
.com/2010/12/architecture-of-black-mountain-college.html:
Figure 1.43

The Country Gentleman, November 1931: Figure 3.1

Town of Huntington, Long Island, Building Department,
demolition permit October 22, 1987: Figure 3.15

*Victoria Newhouse, *Wallace K. Harrison, Architect* (New York:
Rizzoli International, 1989): Figure 3.14

*Walter Gropius, *The New Architecture and the Bauhaus*
(Cambridge, Massachusetts: MIT Press, 1965): Figure 2.20

About the Authors

Frances Campani and Jon Michael Schwarting are a husband-and-wife architect team who have worked for thirty-seven years to save and protect the Aluminaire House and formed the Aluminaire House Foundation for that purpose. They established Campani and Schwarting Architects in 2000. Together, they have experience with many types and scales of work and have completed numerous projects involving new construction, additions, and renovations as well as urban design. Their work is known for its aesthetic distinction, attention to context, and for its innovative use of materials. Frances Campani is an Assistant Professor of Architecture and Jon Michael Schwarting is Professor Emeritus at New York Institute of Technology where the rescue of the Aluminaire House began. Frances Campani and Jon Michael Schwarting live and practice architecture in Port Jefferson, New York.

Frances Campani and Jon Michael Schwarting at the Aluminaire House site in Palm Springs, 2023.

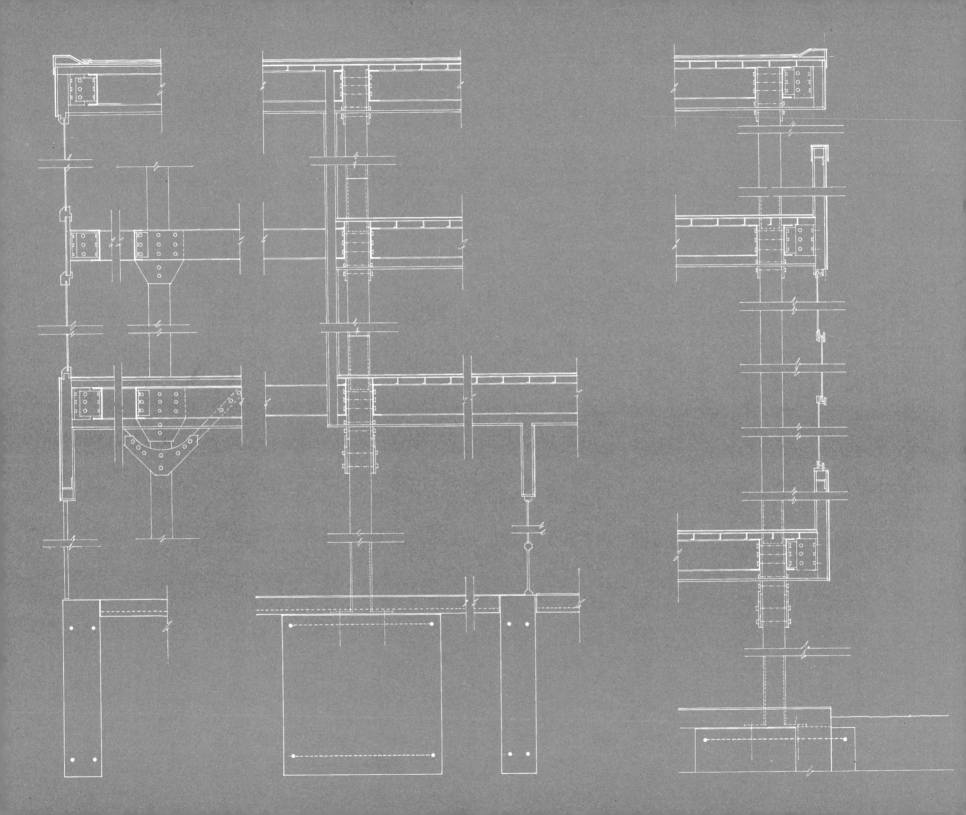